Embracing Intercession

Through Life's Experiences

Embracing Intercession Through Life's Experiences

Copyright © 2015

Author: Shelia Taylor-Pearson

Publishing: Anointed Fire House

Website: www.anointedfirehouse.com

Email: info@anointedfire.com

All scriptures noted in this book were taken from the Amplifiied Bible unless otherwise noted.

ISBN-13: 978-0692436509

ISBN-10: 0692436502

Disclaimer: I have tried to recreate events, locales and conversations from my memories of them. In order to maintain their anonymity in some instances, I have changed the names of individuals and places, I may have changed some identifying characteristics and details such as physical properties, occupations and places of residence.

Although the author and publisher have made every effort to ensure that the information in this book was correct at press time, the author and publisher do not assume and hereby disclaim any liability to any party for any loss, damage, or disruption caused by errors or omissions, whether such errors or omissions result from negligence, accident, or any other cause.

Table of Contents

Introduction

In this book, I will share the prescribed procedure that I
had to walk through to come into contact with who God
created me to be. Through this process, I had to follow all
of God's rules, laws, and directions. It was God's way or
the wilderness way. The wilderness way is walking in
circles, never arriving at your preordained place in life. I
have learned that God is always trying to instruct us. He is
our Compass, and we must position ourselves to know His
specific directions.

Throughout this book, I will share what it means to me
to be processed. I will share how important it is that we
walk only in the direction God is leading us to walk in. We
will be instructed to go in directions that our flesh is totally
against, but we must follow our God given directions.

Being processed means allowing God to prepare you
for the rest of your life. This means allowing Him to
uncover truth about you. I mean, exactly where you are in
every season. God had to walk me back through the good
as well as the bad. He had to uncover mysteries about
things I had suffered in my childhood. The struggles I've

experienced throughout life were identified by God as parts of the process. Before you reach the conclusion of this book, the truth will be revealed to you on a powerful level. You will be given an opportunity to journey with me through a God process. I will share situations and circumstances that shook me back into alignment with God's plan. I will also share experiences that opened my eyes to see and my heart to change. Fault-finding was done away with and I was commanded to see the truth about myself.

Through this process, I was taught the power of a fall, the sifting that comes with the spirit of pride and the levels of elevation you can miss walking in self-righteousness. I will uncover the lessons I've learned, and how they taught me that humility is the only power that exalts. Through all of my ups and downs, failures and disappointments, God has shown me that I was only being processed. I was being shaped and molded into a vessel fit for the Master's use.

Over the years, I have truly learned what being processed consists of. I have walked through many stages of life, only to find who I was created to be. God has given me revelation after revelation about my identity in Him through my own past experiences. My identity was never revealed during the tests, only when I'd successfully walked through them. It always appeared as if God was waiting at the finish line, and then, He would slowly walk me back through the race, explaining every bump, every bruise, and all the pot holes I'd experienced along the way. Throughout this journey, I've learned the importance of endurance. I now understand that God remains silent during the race so that we can come into contact with the endurance He has placed on the inside of us. As intercessors, we must live our lives never giving up. We must know that God is God and He continues to reward those who diligently seek Him.

God has given me an opportunity to share my journey toward becoming a partner with Christ with the whole world, and while on this journey, I have learned that you can't be labeled as an intercessor without suffering. Our Great Intercessor, Jesus Christ, suffered even to the death of the cross. So, as I walk you through my life, you will see me falling and getting back up again. You will also see how those vicious cycles matured me into the woman of God I am now. Through all my life's failures, I've learned endurance. I've learned that every experience I've endured was a process I had to go through so I could become aware of the ambassador that was waiting to come out of me.

I know that all my life's experiences were created that I may truly see through the eyes of God. It wasn't until I learned to stay focused on spiritual matters that my victories became sweat-less ones. God has taken me back as far as my time in the womb of my mother. Through that recap, God has helped me to embrace the life of a prayer warrior: the life that demonstrates standing firm in the

Lord, regardless of the test.

Through it all, I've learned that I must be processed to receive my reward. My surviving everything that was sent to kill me qualifies me to be a spokesperson for the kingdom of God. Regardless of what I had to suffer to arrive at this point, my victory is in the fact that I survived. It doesn't matter what I've lost over the years, no one has the power to take the lessons I've learned. So, partner with me as we journey into a life that prays and never gives up. Go with me as I share the experiences that birthed out the intercessor within.

My Prayer for You

It is my prayer that my journey will help yours. I pray that everything I share in this book will produce fruit in your life. It is God's desire that you be fruitful and multiply. I pray that you will receive the needed information to arrive at your appointed place in life. I pray that humility will continue to be the leading force in your life, and that our Compass (God Himself) will continue to point you in the right direction. I cancel every assignment that Satan has created to abort your destiny. I speak life to you and command your spirit to bring forth fruit like never before. I speak God's order to your feet, and I pray that every step you take will be a sure one. I speak to your fruit and I say multiply in the earth realm. I speak to who you are and I say come forth in Jesus name. I pray that pride and arrogance won't manifest, only humility and the love of

Jesus. Keep your head up and your ears attentive to the voice of God. He is giving you instructions and I command your ears to hear and your spirit to receive.

In Jesus Name,

Amen.

Chapter 1

Preparation for the Journey

And He Who searches the hearts of men knows what is in
the mind of the [Holy] Spirit [what His intent is], because
the Spirit intercedes and pleads [before God] in behalf of
the saints according to and in harmony with God's will.
We are assured and know that [God being a partner in their
labor] all things work together and are [fitting into a plan]
for good to and for those who love God and are called
according to [His] design and purpose (Romans 8:27-28
Amp).

I accepted Jesus as Lord and Savior of my life at the
tender age of twenty. I had just recently given birth to my
first child. During this time, life had come at me with great
force. I had gone through every kind of abuse a woman my
age could handle. I had watched my father abuse my
stepmother, and consequently, I entered into an abusive
relationship. I found myself looking for love and the
enemy made sure I found the counterfeit, the wolf in
sheep's clothing. I'd entered into a very controlling
relationship. I found myself moving according to the
instructions of man, instead of God. My life was very

stressful at an early age, and I had no clue as to how to make it better. But once I met Jesus, instantly, my eyes were opened. I was in such a hot pursuit for change that tarrying for the Holy Ghost was something I didn't have to experience. The day I accepted Jesus was the day His Spirit entered my heart. Even though I was still young, I had gone through some tough stages in my life. I really wanted to know Jesus and I studied His Word and prayed as if it was something I had always done. My desire to talk to Jesus was unbelievable! I spoke to Him everywhere: on my job, in my car, and while I was cooking. I constantly talked to Him. I prayed in the Spirit so much that I heard tongues in my sleep. Praying became my life, and if I didn't pray, I didn't feel like myself.

In the beginning of my new life, I'd attended Agape Storge Christian Center and it was a fairly large ministry. I was trying my best to embrace newness and it was very difficult to go to anyone with my problems. I was very good at repenting for constant sin and starting over again. I had accepted Jesus, but I was still bound by the issues of life. I was very strong when it came to talking to God, but I hadn't quite tapped into the principle of knowing the voice of God. I was good at releasing life's situations through my emotions. I was never still enough or stable enough to wait on God's instructions. I found myself running from life's situations instead of allowing God to build me up in the

things of the Spirit. Because of this, I made major
decisions without hearing from Him. I will never forget the
season I visited Vessels of Mercy Church. There was a
great pull on me to join this ministry, but I hadn't quite
made the decision to walk according to God's standard of
holiness. I was still enjoying my worldly lifestyle, and
there was something about this church that placed a
command on me to live holy. I was having too much fun
doing what I wanted to do and serving God when I felt like
it. I was the type of believer who lived a lukewarm
lifestyle. I wasn't quite ready to live holy, but I couldn't
stay out of the atmosphere that Vessels of Mercy Church
introduced. I will never forget the way God dealt with me
concerning my lifestyle. I visited the church when the
atmosphere was filled with God's glory and everyone had
uplifted hands, but when I attempted to worship God with
my hands lifted, a force kept pushing them down. I could
literally feel myself fighting to worship God. The more I
attempted to raise my hands, the stronger this invisible
force became. The presence of God felt so good and very
inviting, but Satan was enjoying my then lukewarm body
and wasn't quite ready to give it up. I wanted to really
experience the presence of God on another level, and I was
willing to fight the devil to receive from God. I fought
until something demonic began to manifest through my
body. I found myself on the floor, wiggling like a snake. I
had no control of my body, and I could hear people around

me commanding this spirit to come out. The people of God were speaking in tongues and laying hands like I had never seen.

God showed me in a very powerful way that I couldn't play church. He would rather that you be cold or hot than to be lukewarm. At that very moment, I chose Jesus for real. I feared God, and I didn't want anything to do with the devil. The Bible tells us that sinners shall not stand in the congregation of the righteous and God really proved that to me. Psalms 1:5-6 (Amp) states, "Therefore the wicked [those disobedient and living without God] shall not stand [justified] in the judgment, nor sinners in the congregation of the righteous [those who are upright and in right standing with God]. For the Lord knows and is fully acquainted with the way of the righteous, but the way of the ungodly [those living outside God's will] shall perish (end in ruin and come to naught)."

I had made the decision to live holy, but I still wasn't quite ready to obey God completely. He was leading me to join Vessels of Mercy Church, but I had other plans. I was so tired of my home town and was ready to see and experience other things, but I was looking for change in all the wrong places. We can only find newness in the Spirit; the Bible lets us know that there is nothing new under the sun. So, I was seeking for something in the natural that I could only receive in the Spirit. I rejected the Spirit and embraced the natural by moving to Georgia with my older sister. I want you to notice that I made the decision, not God. The Bible encourages us, in Proverbs 3:5-6 (Amp), to lean on, trust in, and be confident in the Lord with all our hearts and minds, and do not rely on our own insight or understandings. In all our ways, we are to know, recognize, and acknowledge Him, and He will direct and make straight and plain our paths.

I moved to Georgia with a plan, but not with a God given plan. I enrolled in the Beulah Heights Bible College. During this time, I really had a strong zeal to pastor my own church. Notice, I was making adjustments in my life to become a pastor and I hadn't begun to face the trials I would have to face on this journey with God. After moving with my sister for only a few months, everything I had envisioned began to vanish. My sister and I ended up homeless, staying in a hotel for weeks. I couldn't pay my car note because I needed to use that money to find a place to live. All I could see taking place in my life was trial after trial. My sister and I eventually got an apartment and shared the rent and utilities. We stayed together for a few months until she decided to get her own house, so I ended up stuck with rent I couldn't afford and working double shifts at least three times a week to get the bills paid. *Talk about getting out of God's will for your life!* After being in my apartment for nearly four months, my car was repossessed. I was left in a big city with no transportation, an apartment that was too much for me to handle, and I was too prideful to return home. I knew that I had made a bad decision when it came to making that move. I also knew that I had to seek God out of a pure heart for my life to get better.

I had gone through as much as I could take, and I knew that things had to get better. But, to my surprise, the trials had just begun and would grow worse if I didn't walk in God's perfect will for my life. One day, my other sister and her friend surprised me with a knock on my door. I was trying my best to take care of my own personal issues when my sister showed up to live with me with no resources. My cry was, "Oh, Lord, what's next?" It was really time for me to hear from God. I was fed up, and now, the time had come for me to pull down pride and put on humbleness of mind. I made it through that year, but as soon as the next year rolled in, I rolled out. I bought a new car, filled it with gas, and headed back home. It was time to close that chapter of my life and allow God to give me better chapters.

I had to allow the Spirit of God to take me through a process of taking things out. I returned home excited about being delivered from everything I had faced in Georgia.

Preparation for the Journey

The warfare was very intense and the journey was long, but I made it through. I reached a season in my life that I had to allow God to take me through a purifying process. I was back home and was looking forward to joining the church of God's choice. I didn't waste time joining my best friend's church. Shortly after I joined Vessels of Mercy, I accepted my call as a minister of the Gospel. I had run from the call long enough, and the time had come to obey the voice of God. I went to the pastor drenched in sweat and tears, knowing that lives were depending on me to obey. Once the call and announcement was made, more tests and trials began. I believe every demonic force came against me. I began to understand why God had to establish me in a strong prayer life. It took me having a strong prayer life to maintain my joy.

Shortly after I accepted my call to the ministry, God used my new pastor to open my eyes to another level of prayer. He explained to me that I was an intercessory prayer leader. He put so much excitement in me that I began to invest in books and tapes, anything I could get my hands on concerning intercessory prayer. I was very excited about knowing my purpose and embraced it with all of my heart. It wasn't long before God put me on my first prayer assignment. The Lord revealed to me that my ministry started with my mother and sister. It wasn't until I settled down and got rid of my own selfish desires that God began to line my life up with His perfect will.

I really have a strong zeal to do the work of the Lord. I am also aware of the strong call that I have on my life, but I still have to flow with the Spirit of God. I have to allow Him to prepare me for this life-long journey. Moving to Georgia and attending Bible College seemed like a great start at the time, but it wasn't God's will for my life. I know that my assignment is great, but I must get the job done God's way. We can't step outside of God's will and think that He's going to continue to give us directions. There is no way we can accidentally enter into God's will walking in the wrong direction. Jesus is our High Priest, and we must follow His instructions. We must flow in God's timing, not our own. One move caused my whole life to be full of turmoil. I realize that time is precious, and we must always do things in God's timing and in God's way.

Putting First Things First

FIRST OF all, then, I admonish and urge that petitions, prayers, intercessions, and thanksgivings be offered on behalf of all men, For kings and all who are in positions of authority or high responsibility, that [outwardly] we may pass a quiet and undisturbed life [and inwardly] a peaceable one in all godliness and reverence and seriousness in every way. For such [praying] is good and right, and [it is] pleasing and acceptable to God our Savior. Who wishes all men to be saved and [increasingly] to perceive and recognize and discern and know precisely and correctly the [divine] Truth (1 Timothy 2:1-4 Amp).

God has given us His Son, Jesus Christ, to empower us to live victorious lives. He has given us the authority to build up the kingdom of God, but we must be prepared for this life-long journey. It is vital that we walk in the commandments of God, putting first Him first. Apostle Paul admonishes the body of Christ to make petitions unto the Lord. This level of praying places us in a position of acknowledging our position through the shed blood of Christ. We now can come boldly to the throne of grace. Our acknowledgment of Christ's finished work places us in a position of maturity. It demonstrates a transition from death to life, giving us the benefits of entering into the fullness of God's grace and abundant love. Now that the blood has run its course, we can pray to the Father through the Son. Prayer can come forth only when we know that He is God. The realm of intercession introduces to us the spirit of diligence. You must move out of the natural *(praying according to your emotions and will)* and move into the spirit *(praying according to God's will)*. Intercession rewards us with the very presence of who we're praying to. We come into intimate contact with the true and living God Who rewards those who diligently seek Him. Intercession doesn't just pray to God, but it releases

God. It has the power to transform us into carriers of His glory. It changes us from just being saved into being true spiritual temples, abiding places for His holy presence. Intercession walks us out of the flesh and into the Spirit. Through intercession, a cleansing takes place, and once we've been purified through a holy washing, we are led into the presence of a Holy King. And once we've experienced the presence of God, we become living sanctuaries, abiding places for God, birthing channels that release God's will into the earth realm.

The release of intercession does not eliminate the test and trials that are bound to occur in our lives. Challenges will come. There are things that will present themselves to us constantly; whether it's our family, our finances, or simply our communities and cities. These things are shown to us because we have the ability to release change. Change starts only when we realize that the source of the problem is coming from an invisible enemy. Intercession teaches us that every challenge must be viewed through the eyes of God. We are created in the image of God and His Spirit. So, we must operate in the Spirit to truly represent God in the earth realm. Through this powerful work of God, we are given the ability to see our spiritual opponent and deal with him in the realm of the supernatural. We can only fight a spiritual enemy in the spirit. Satan understands that his kingdom advances more and more when we fail to embrace truth. Our lack of knowledge keeps us in bondage, even though Jesus died that we may be free. It is time we walk in the fullness of God by putting on our spiritual eyes so we can really deal with our spiritual enemy.

I now understand why it is a must that we walk in the Spirit. Flesh has the ability to chain us down and eat at us until we die spiritually. It is like a cancer. If we don't catch the problem in time, it destroys us. It is time we deal with life situations in the realm of the spirit, and it is a must that we abide there. Since I've been in the school of prayer, God has shown me how powerful the flesh really is. It is a selfish, prideful part of the human being. It is the part of us that craves for more of the world, and it is designed to get us completely off God's course. To deal with our fleshy nature, we must draw into God's presence on a more serious level, and it is vital that we abide there.

Being Persistent in Prayer

Do not, therefore, fling away your fearless confidence, for it carries a great and glorious compensation of reward. For you have need of steadfast patience and endurance, so that you may perform and fully accomplish the will of God, and thus receive and carry away [and enjoy to the full] what is promised (Hebrews 10:35-36 Amp).

Preparation for the Journey is a chapter that will teach you the importance of being persistent in prayer. Prayer is the force that prepares us for a life of walking and pleasing our heavenly Father. I can't repeat this enough: prayer does not eliminate the tests and trials in your life. But I can assure you that if you remain steadfast in the things of God, everything will work together for your good. Prayer keeps you under the covering of the power of God. The Bible tells us in Psalm 91:1 (Amp) that he who dwells in the secret place of the Most High shall remain stable and fixed under the shadow of the Almighty [Whose power no foe can withstand]. As you can see, once you decide to put prayer in its rightful place, God will forever keep you under His protected power.

In God's presence, everything that concerns us must line up with the Word of God. And getting our gaze right is essential; it is a must that we see truth. God is truly waiting on a people who will hearken to His commandments. He is waiting on a people who do not mind going into the realm of the spirit and taking what rightfully belongs to them. It is time we take on a warfare mentality, killing everything that does not line up with the Word. It is time we command everything that concerns us to line up with the Word of God. I'm convinced that once we open our mouths to release God's Word into the earth realm, everything will stand in attention. The Bible lets us know that every knee must bow at the name of Jesus. So our obedience in releasing His name will always deliver amazing results.

I mentioned earlier in this chapter how my ministry started with my mother and sister. During this time, my mother had an alcohol addiction and my sister had cancer. At that time, I didn't understand why my first assignment was so hard, but I understand now that the Lord wanted to teach me persistence. God had revealed to me that the enemy wanted to kill them and it was my job, as an intercessor, to cover them. God didn't give me the assignment because they were my family, but the Lord was letting me know that the assignment was 100% spiritual, and I had to go into it with a spiritual mind.

I accepted the assignment, and daily ministered healing to my sister and deliverance to my mother. I explained to them what they would have to do to maintain their healing and deliverance. I talked with them on a daily basis, trying my best to increase their faith, and in the process, make my assignment a little easier. During this time, I didn't understand the fullness of the call, and the assignment was getting the best of me. I now understand that the Lord wanted me to pray for them and to fight in the spirit, but instead, I allowed surface matters to shift me. During this time, I was working overtime in my own home. I would release the Word and pray in the comfort of my mother's home daily. I was very bold in the spirit and dealing with the devil became the norm. My mother had a heart to change and looked forward to me ministering to her. I would encourage my family on a regular basis. Besides, they were my assignment, and as long as I stayed focused on that, change manifested.

The minute I began to slack in ministry, the enemy gained ground in my life. I became too busy to visit my mother and sister, and when I did show up, I saw that the enemy and his entire host had invaded my territory. When I became out of balance, the enemy returned home, and home, to him, was the bodies of my mother and sister. The Bible states, "But when the unclean spirit has gone out of a man, it roams through dry [arid] places in search of rest, but it does not find any. Then it says, I will go back to my house from which I came out. And when it arrives, it finds the place unoccupied, swept, put in order, and decorated. Then it goes and brings with it seven other spirits more wicked than itself, and they go in and make their home there. And the last condition of that man becomes worse than the first. So also shall it be with this wicked generation (See Matthew 12: 43-45 Amp).

I can still recall how sick I felt the next time I saw my mother and sister. The Bible teaches us that the weapons of our warfare are not carnal, but mighty through God to the pulling down of strongholds….. (2 Corinthians 10:4). Instead of fighting in the spirit, I was trying to handle a spiritual problem in the natural. I had become so caught up in my emotions that I stopped going around them. I became so disgusted with what my natural eyes saw that I completely gave up on the assignment.

The key to being persistent in this life as an intercessor is realizing that we can't deal with spiritual matters with a carnal mindset. I couldn't convince my mother to stop drinking and I couldn't convince my sister to believe God for her healing. My job was to pray that the chains of bondage be broken off my family. I had to pray that the enemy's veil be loosed from their eyes and that God would give them eyes to see. My job was to bind the works of the devil in Jesus name. God wanted me to call heaven down to work on their behalf. Jesus informs us in St. Matthew 18:18 (Amp) that whatever we forbid and declare to be improper and unlawful on earth must be what is already forbidden in heaven, and whatever we permit and declare proper and lawful on earth must be what is already permitted in heaven. God wanted me to declare that the attacks from the enemy were improper and would not be tolerated.

Tragedy hit my life less than a year after disobeying

my God given assignment. My sister died shortly after I'd gotten married, and my mother died shortly after I had given birth to my youngest daughter. They passed exactly three and half months apart, and losing them tapped me into a life of praying until victory is won. Through the loss of my family, I learned that lives are depending on us to be persistent. It is vital that we remain focused on the assignment God gives us. Obedience is so much better than sacrifice. I beat myself up because I knew that I hadn't gone into the assignment with the power God had vested in me, but losing my mother and sister caused me to be a better person and a stronger intercessor. In the beginning, Luke 8:14 described me, "And that which fell among thorns are they, which, when they have heard, go forth, and are choked with cares and riches and pleasures of life, and bring no fruit to perfection." But after losing my mother and sister months apart, Luke 8:15 describes who I am now and who I will forever be. "But that on good ground are they, which in an honest and good heart having heard the word keep it and bring forth fruit with patience." Losing them has given me the ability to bring forth fruit with patience. I miss them so much, and even though they're not here with me, they are yet leading me into a life that prays and never gives up until victory is won.

My Prayer for You
It is my prayer that you will allow God to prepare you for

the journey. I pray that you will live a surrendered life, allowing God's Spirit to lead and guide you into all truth. It is God's desire that you know His voice, and the voice of a stranger, you will never follow. I pray that God will fine tune your ears, giving you the supernatural ability to hear His voice. I pray that God will bring order to your steps, and that everything that concerns you will line up with His perfect will. I speak to your purpose, commanding your spirit to pick up the pace according to God's timetable. And I stop every satanic assignment sent to hinder your progress in the kingdom. God is waiting on an opportune moment to bring you into His promises, and I push you into your place of destiny, free of distractions. I pray that every move you make will be a God move, and everything that the enemy attempted to do to you is aborted in the spirit now. I kill the seed of Satan, and I speak manifestations unto every positive word God has spoken concerning you. God is on your side, and if God is for you, who can be against you? I pray that you bring forth fruit with patience, allowing God to increase your faith on a daily basis. Look up and know that no weapon formed against you will ever prosper. I pray that you remain in the spirit, never looking at the things that are seen because the battle is always in the unseen realm. In Jesus name, I pray that you will stay focused, allowing God to reconstruct your very life. It is God's desire that you move into the things of Him, free of worldly distractions and staying on a clear path. He wants

17

you to walk into your promised land demonstrating your ability to stand through every test. So, I speak, therefore, to you: Stand in God in Jesus name!

Chapter 2

Living a Balanced Life

Do nothing from fractional motives [through contentiousness, strife, selfishness, or for unworthy ends] or prompted by conceit and empty arrogance. Instead in the true spirit of humility (lowliness of mind) let each regard the others as better than and superior to himself [thinking more highly of one another than you do of yourselves] (Philippians 2:3 Amp).

The Lord has given us everything we need to maintain balance. On the other hand, we must also remain aware of our adversary, the devil. He works overtime, doing everything in his power to hinder God's plan for our lives. Staying tuned in to the direction of the Holy Spirit is vital in this walk with Christ. The enemy is always on his job, and he never comes short of his plans. It is our jobs as Christ's representatives to counteract those plans. Remaining stable enough to get all of God's instructions is crucial in every season. We should never be carried away by the dictates of our human nature.

It is Satan's job to break our focus. He specializes in

targeting our spiritual gaze. A spiritual gaze keeps us on
the path that leads to the promises of God. We must know
that Satan is the god of this world, and he knows just what
to do to get us off course. This reminds me of the time I
accepted my husband's proposal. I had recently accepted
my call to the ministry, and God was really uncovering
some serious things to me concerning my life's assignment.
I was very excited about taking this wonderful news to my
pastor. My pastor questioned me concerning my fiancé's
lifestyle, and honestly, I felt that my fiancé's life wasn't any
of his business. He was trying everything in his power to
convince me that this was not the will of God for my life.
At the time, I was too caught up on the fact that my fiancé
loved me and didn't mind demonstrating it. I had gladly
accepted the proposal and had no intentions of going
against my word. I was convinced that my pastor was out
of line and I had the right to make my own decisions.
Besides, it was my life and not my pastor's. I wouldn't
allow his advice to take root in my spirit. I left my church
in a very bad, haughty, and arrogant spirit. I left the church
with the intentions of never looking back. I'd allowed my
emotions to dominate me in that situation. I walked away,
convincing myself that I was right and he was completely
wrong. Yes, it was my life and I had the right to make the
final decisions for my life, but it was also my job to respect
his counsel and allow God to line my life up according to
His perfect will. I then moved to Memphis, Tennessee,

regretting everything I had released toward my pastor. I
knew that he couldn't take away my will to decide and I
should have respected his position as a leader. I ended up
moving to Memphis full of bitterness and anger. I allowed
months to pass before even attempting to find a new church
home. Once I started working, I met a lady who was on
fire for God. She came to work every week talking about
how the Spirit moved in her church. I was convinced that
the Lord was using her to direct me to my new church
home. She attended Faith Heritage C.O.G.I.C., and I was
somewhat stuck on the fact that I had a non-denominational
background. So, I was really hesitant about even visiting
her church, but eventually, she'd convinced me to go. After
attending a few services, the Spirit of God prompted me to
join. Once I'd joined Faith Heritage, I would always sit
near the back, praying that the Lord wouldn't reveal to the
man and woman of God that I had a call on my life, but
during each service, the first lady would invite me to sit
with the leaders. I knew then that the Lord had revealed
my secret. In obedience, I sat with them, and I could
literally feel the Spirit of God breaking me. Finally, I
explained my situation to the first lady and God used her to
minister to my heart. She explained the importance of me
repenting for being disrespectful to the man of God. She
told me that I had to get things right to continue growing in
this walk with Christ. Shortly after I'd humbled myself,
God began to purify my way of thinking, and He brought

balance into my life. Once we humble ourselves enough to see our shortcomings and repent, the Lord instantly begins to line our lives up with His perfect will. We have to position ourselves to receive from God. Our human nature tells us that we can do things our own way. We must learn to crucify our flesh and allow God to be God in our lives. It is time we embrace the fact that even though we were born into sin, we do not have to remain in sin. We can now live a life of thanking God for the blood of the Lamb who was wounded for our transgressions and bruised for our iniquities (see Isaiah 53:5). Yes, we can now walk complete in Christ, applying His Word to every aspect of our lives.

It is very important that we come to Jesus with a broken and contrite heart, realizing that we need Him to purify our ways of thinking. Once we repent, we have to know that all things are working out, even when it seems like nothing is making sense. I can remember not fully understanding why God wanted me to connect with this particular church. I felt that a lot of things that God had revealed to me concerning my life's assignment didn't line up 100% with their organization. I now know that God was using this phase in my life to humble me. It really took me putting my flesh under subjection to remain a part of this ministry. My first lady was someone I really admired. I had an opportunity to grow in wisdom in a very personal and powerful way. God really used her to mature me in the things of Him. There wasn't anything that I asked her that didn't evoke her wisdom to spring forth. I had no idea that the Lord was using this ministry to bring balance into my life. I was granted the opportunity to attend Bible College, and I also had the privilege of being ordained by some of the most anointed people in the world. Nevertheless, I began to feel like nothing in my life made sense. I had completed everything that was required of me, but it seemed as if I had lost my zeal during the process. I couldn't understand why I didn't have the same passion I'd always had for the ministry. I couldn't deny the growth: I had grown tremendously in the things of God. The Lord allowed me the opportunity to sit and be fed by this man and woman of God for four years, and I felt honored to have had the privilege to be counseled by such a powerful man and woman of God.

During this season of my life, I didn't know what to do, so I turned completely to the Word of God. I began to apply Psalms 37:3-7 (Amp) to my life on a daily basis. It states, "Trust (lean on, rely on, and be confident) in the Lord and do good; so shall you dwell in the land and feed surely on His faithfulness, and truly you shall be fed. Delight yourself also in the Lord, and He will give you the desires and secret petitions of your heart. Commit your way to the Lord [roll and repose each care of your load on

Him]; trust (lean on, rely on, and be confident also in Him and He will bring it to pass." Regardless of how I felt during this time of my life, I had to trust in the Lord and do good. I never allowed anyone to know exactly how I felt about leaving my home church to become a part of the Church of God in Christ. I remained faithful, serving in the ministry, and God began to show me myself. He showed me how prejudiced I was concerning the things of Him.

Prejudice, according to Dictionary.com, is *an unfavorable opinion or feeling formed beforehand or without knowledge or reason.* I had never attended this type of ministry, nor had I done research on the history of it. I would have missed out on everything God wanted to do in that season had I allowed a spirit of prejudice to prevail. God began to show me all the boundaries I had placed on Him. Becoming a part of the Church of God in Christ really brought balance to my life. I now realize that God is *too big* for our boundaries. We get stuck on denominations or non-denominations, but God is not moved by our small thinking. It is so important that we don't allow our limited thinking to limit the power God desires to release through us. There are demonstrations of His power that He's waiting to release in this earth realm, but we must take the boundaries off! For me to become the leader I was born to be, I must remain humble under the mighty hands of God. He knew all about me and He also knew the process I needed to take to get some stability in my life. God used a powerful denominational ministry to discipline me in the things of Him, a ministry I wouldn't have chosen at that time because of my limited thinking.

God is waiting on an opportunity to elevate His people, but we must first become one body. The Lord is not coming back for titles or denominations, but He is coming back that He might present the church to Himself in glorious splendor, without spot or wrinkle or any such things (see Ephesians 5:27). It is time for the church to take the boundaries off God and allow Him to move freely in this earth realm. The enemy uses these boundaries to keep division in the body of Christ. He understands that a house divided against itself shall not stand (see Matthew 12:25). Apostle Paul encourages us in 1 Corinthians 1:10 (Amp) to come together as one. It states, "But I urge and entreat you, brethren, by the name of our Lord Jesus Christ, that all of you be in perfect harmony and full agreement in what you say, and that there be no dissensions or factions of divisions among you, but that you be perfectly united in your common understanding and in your opinions and judgments." God has called and anointed me to bring His people back into true Biblical intercession. The enemy knew that as long as I put boundaries on the move of the Spirit, I wouldn't tap into the fullness of the call. I now realize that God is in control of my life and He can do whatever He wants, whenever He wants, and however He wants to do it. As intercessors, we must learn to live surrendered lives. God must have free course to move us into different dimensions in the spirit.

Humility Exalts

Whoever exalts himself [with haughtiness and empty pride] shall be humble (brought low), and whoever humble himself [who ever has a modest opinion of himself and behaves accordingly] shall be raised to honor (St. Matthew 23:12 Amp).

I can testify that God truly corrects those whom He loves. God had to take out my filthy way of thinking to line my life up with His perfect will. I had to humble myself to see myself. After God revealed to me that I didn't have His way of thinking, He began to do a transformation in my mind. Once my thoughts began to line up with God's Word, my life began to line up with God's will. He revealed to me that I had an assignment at my home church and within the city. During this time, God had just ordained me for ministry and He didn't release me to tell anyone except my sister. The assignment was so vital that God began to tap me into my pastor's warfare. I then called and explained to him that God had revealed to me that it was time for me to return home to his ministry.

Before moving home, God had me to read *Seasons of Intercession* by Frank Damazio. I was amazed at how God began to give me instructions through this man of God. I knew that I was in Memphis, Tennessee, but God was giving me a work to do in Greenville, Mississippi. After reading *Seasons of Intercession*, I knew that there was no way I could receive what God had for me if I remained in Memphis. God knew that these instructions wouldn't make sense to a natural mind. I had come to realize that God was ready to bring me into a life of abundance, and I couldn't share this revelation with anyone.

God used Pastor Frank Damazio's book to paint a mental picture of my life's assignment. The Lord was calling me to give myself to the things of the spirit until it changes things in the natural. I had to position myself, allowing the Holy Spirit to reveal what the enemy was doing in the realm of the spirit. God was calling me to teach others the importance of building hedges around people, houses, marriages, children, churches, cities, and regions. God was concerned about the city of Greenville, and His instructions were strategic. I knew, without a shadow of doubt, that God was calling strong intercessors to seek out the gaps in the wall. He was calling for a rebuilding of the walls in Greenville, Mississippi.

Through Mr. Damazio's obedience in writing *Seasons*

of Intercession, I was about to step boldly into my preordained assignment. God empowered me to bring churches together all over the city. He positioned me to release His Spirit in the city through a call to repentance, unifying the churches and establishing strategic levels of intercession. I was called and anointed to put prayer back in its rightful place in my hometown. My main assignment was to unify corporate prayer with the churches in the city of Greenville. God had a plan to counter the works of the devil and I was now aware of the assignment. I was informed and ready to go forth, but I had one question for God: *How can I explain this to my husband?* We had been living in Memphis for years, and he'd never mentioned moving back home. God commanded me to remain quiet about His instructions and He would do all the maneuvering.

Shortly after God instructed me not to say anything to my husband, He began to move through my obedience. The doors that were once opened to us began to close. In the midst of trying times, God began to bring the vision to pass. During this time, my husband and I weren't getting along. We were really struggling in a lot of areas of our marriage, and living in Memphis had become difficult. I believe that my husband did everything in his power to remain in Memphis, but the best decision was to return home. Once I allowed God to cleanse me from all unrighteousness, He showed me a clear path. Through my obedience in returning home, God began moving in extreme ways. He increased my faith, gave me more vision, and empowered me to run. Regardless of how I felt about the Church of God in Christ, God proved that He is God. Everything I've gone through, every word of wisdom, everything I've put my hands to do in the Faith Heritage Church of God in Christ prepared me for the rest of my life. I humbled myself, saw the darkness in my heart, repented, and God exalted me.

It really took God imparting a spirit of humility in me to get me to move in synchronization with His movement. I knew I had to follow all of God's instructions for my life to line up according to His perfect will. I have learned that if you are called to do anything for God's kingdom, He will forever test your heart. We can't begin to imagine how important it is that we stay in a humbled state of mind, showing forth the love of God at all times. It doesn't matter what we have to face in this life, we must express who God is on a daily basis.

After returning home, I started back serving in Vessels of Mercy Church. As you can see, I hadn't completed what God wanted me to do in this church, but I was thankful for another chance. It wasn't long before God showed me how the spirit of pride attaches itself to the people of God. I can remember one Sunday when my sister and I were really enjoying church service, but it appeared to others that we were playing. Shortly after service, an usher corrected us. Taking correction from an usher was completely humiliating to me. Instantly, I reacted in the flesh and felt that I had to let her know she was out of line for correcting ministers of the Gospel. I wasn't aware of how wrong I was until my pastor openly rebuked me. I felt very badly about the rebuke, and I couldn't understand why he'd handled the situation the way he did, but the Lord ministered to me about how important it was that I let nothing kill my witness. God used my pastor to correct me Saturday morning during intercessory prayer, and Sunday after service, I was in his office thanking him for handling me in that regard. Once God places us in a position of authority, it is very important that we don't allow a spirit of pride to come into our hearts.

The Lord expects us to stay humble at all times. This can be easy in the beginning of our new life with Christ, but over the years, humility may prove hard to maintain. Once God begins to manifest His holy boldness in us, it is vital that we maintain humble. The enemy works continuously to take our eyes off the real battle. He understands God is teaching us to war only in spiritual battles. The open rebuke caused me to see the real problem: I had gotten off balance in my walk of humility with God. I now realize that I can't allow anything to damage my character, and at all times, I must walk in the integrity of God. It doesn't matter how anointed we become, we must imitate the One who has given us this power. We must live our lives to walk in love, joy, peace, longsuffering, gentleness, faith, meekness, and temperance.

To walk complete in Christ, we must allow the spirit of humility to manifest in our lives. We must strip ourselves of our own selfish desires and walk in complete harmony with the Spirit of God. This will take us abasing ourselves to the fullest and allowing God to have complete control. Jesus is greater than anything we will ever have to face in this life, and He expects us to demonstrate His greatness.

I would like to share another one of my life's experiences to show you how God continues to test us in the area of humility. I was approached by one of the leaders at my church, and she had a very haughty spirit. She talked very badly to me, walking away and screaming that my ministry would burn. I knew that she didn't approach me in the Spirit of Christ, even though she was in a position of leadership. I knew that the enemy was using her, and God revealed to me that the spirit of pride was being manifested in her life. He instructed me to go and apologize to her. He wanted the spirit of humility to be exalted above everything the enemy was attempting to do. He also explained that the spirit of pride wasn't going to allow her to apologize to me. I knew that God was ready to take me to another level in Him, and humility will exalt you every time. I went and apologized to her, and I encouraged her to correct me anytime she felt I needed to be corrected. I hugged her and told her I loved her. Now, there's no way this would have taken place if I would have allowed a spirit of pride to prevail. I humbled myself to the fullest, and God immediately exalted me in the realm of the spirit.

My Prayer for You

My prayer for you today is that you will truly live a balanced life, a rich and productive life that allows humility to prevail. I pray that no attempt of the devil will hinder your progress in life, and everything you attempt to do for God's kingdom will advance in a very supernatural way. I pray your life will draw many souls into the kingdom of God, and that you will give those souls a strong desire to live holy and fruitful lives. I pray your walk will demonstrate righteousness on extreme levels, and that you will allow God's Word to be released through you with signs and wonders following. I pray that you will be a true demonstration of God in the earth realm, and that you will release everything He represents, regardless of the tests and trials that will come your way.

In Jesus Name,

Amen.

Chapter 3

Applying Truth Changes Things

And ye shall know the truth and the truth shall make you free (St. John 8:32).

For years, my emotions were the dominating forces that controlled my life, and this caused the spirit of pride to manifest on a very powerful level. I know that pride kept me from the manifestations of God's promises for years. God only brings things to pass when humility becomes a lifestyle for the believer. The opposite of humility is pride, and a spirit of pride holds you captive. There is no way you can reach your full potential if you walk in pride. The enemy does all he can to keep you chained down. He loves bringing up hurtful and painful reminders. His goal is to keep you bound with the issues of life, causing you to never step into your purpose. Purpose is a set goal or aim, and to reach that goal, you must move in the right direction.

Let me share an experience with you that moved me in every direction except the right one. I missed hearing from God when I went into a ministry sounding like people instead of sounding like God. I missed God when I allowed man's doctrine to penetrate my heart instead of the Word of God. Deliverance takes place only when you can see that you have allowed the enemy to blind you to truth. The truth is the only power that can rescue you from the accuser of the brethren. I missed heaven when I looked at man as the visionary instead of God as the Visionary. I must be truthful with myself. I stepped into purpose with my focus on man instead of God. I didn't keep my eyes on the Author and the Finisher of my faith. I embraced purpose depending on a man, and when that man fell short of God's glory, my emotions caused me to let go of purpose. If I would have stayed focused on the One who has begun a good work in me, I wouldn't have been tossed around by every wind of doctrine.

It is important that we know that God is the Visionary. Yes, He empowers man to bring His vision to pass, but God is the Author and Finisher of our faith. We must step into our divine purposes with our minds fixed on God. He is a God of love, and regardless of the tests, He will forever direct us. My assignment for intercessory prayer is God's gift to the world. As long as I remain focused on that fact, man can't stop me. It is vital that we know truth. Truth has the power to uncover layers of darkness and rebuke every glare of dimness. Truth brings you into the very presence of God, causing you to run only in the right direction. We must truly walk in the things of the Spirit to receive God's instructions. We must also position ourselves so we can fully understand God's process.

The Lord sent me back home with a powerful assignment. I relocated full of zeal and fire, waiting on the next move of God. I knew I was to rejoin my home church. After obeying God, within months, God gave me fruit I wouldn't have ever dreamed of possessing.

Shortly after rejoining my home church, I became the intercessory prayer leader. I had a position but no one to lead. During this time, the pastor desired to have a behind the scenes group of prayer warriors. So, God gave me a plan of meeting with a group of believers called The Call Me Indeed Group. I had given my number out to several members, asking them to call me, and shortly thereafter, a meeting time was established. Over thirty members of the church gathered in the fellowship hall. I then announced that it was a call for intercession and briefly explained the role of an intercessor. After sharing my request, only ten members were interested in becoming more knowledgeable about intercession. So, I typed a letter to the pastors, requesting a set time to teach. Weeks later, a school of prayer was established. I taught six sessions on intercession. In the seventh week, the church held an ordination service, and the ten intercessors proudly received their certificates of completion. It was amazing how fast the manifestation of the vision surfaced. I was truly operating in my intercessory prayer gifting.

I was very excited about how rapidly God was moving in my life. It was amazing how things were flowing just the way He had promised. My extreme excitement caused me to become blind to the things God had anointed me to detect. I had finally been given an opportunity to release what had been screaming to come out of me for years. This was a great season for me, but it required serious warfare. I had gone to another level in God, and many doors of opportunity had opened wide for me, but I failed to remember that with those opened doors came many adversaries. I was sure that I was called to be a prayer warrior, but I lost focus of what being a prayer warrior consisted of. The Bible encourages us to, "Be well balanced (temperate, sober of mind), be vigilant and cautious at all times; for the enemy of yours, the devil, roams around like a lion roaring [in fierce hunger], seeking someone to seize upon and devour (see 1 Peter 5:8 Amp)." I had let my guards down and the enemy was hitting me on every side. He was attacking my ministry, finances, children, and my marriage. Instead of fighting, I ran in the opposite direction. I lost focus and ran for my life, or at least, that is what I initially believed. In truth, I was running away from my life. I allowed my natural side to lead me, but God was merciful. I left the church once again full of my emotions. I now realize that I took my eyes off the things of the spirit, therefore, I wasn't prepared for the next level of blows. God was trying to prepare me for the rest of the journey. The battle I was facing was 100% part of the process. The enemy attacked me with his best arsenal in a season that I was too tired to fight back. My fatigued state caused me to turn an unprotected area to the enemy: my back. I ran instead of standing with the firm footed stability I knew I had within me.

God sent me back home to release everything He represents. He had given me the ability to see and hear things others would overlook. My job was to remain sensitive to the Spirit of God so He would release change in the atmosphere. Instead of remaining steadfast in the things of God, I began to allow the atmosphere to change me, and this was a *very bad* decision! God knew what He had given me to do, and He continued to use the leaders in the city to build my faith.

I was given the opportunity to meet two pastors who were anointed to help me put my life back into perspective, and they were the instruments God used in that season to point me back in the right direction. When I met them, my entire life was full of chaos. I had run from an assigned purpose in ministry and was too emotional to step out and obey God when it came to my assignment. *Oh, how I allowed my flesh to mislead me!* I connected with this new ministry for one reason, and that was to get built up enough to walk in my ordained assignment. I was so tired of flesh, and I was fed up with being handled wrongly by leadership. All I wanted to do was obey God. I was being damaged in crazy ways and I found myself constantly running instead of doing ministry. I now know that the hurt I'd experienced was assigned to try me in that particular season of my life. God had to show me the things that needed to be improved in my life. He cared about me so much, He permitted me to fellowship and grow for four months at New Living Way Church. Becoming a part of New Living Way Church introduced me to a whole new dimension. It was an atmosphere soaked with the presence of God, people who craved for a deeper revelation of God, and Words of wisdom pierced the minds of believers. I couldn't believe the dimension in the spirit I was embarking upon. I had an opportunity to fellowship with my new leaders, and they were truly a demonstration of God's character. They loved God's people and didn't mind demonstrating it.

My co-pastor stirred my spirit each time she brought forth the spoken Word. The Lord really released His power through my new found spiritual leaders. I made it top priority to support them every chance I was given. My spirit was hungry for the power that was released through the man and woman of God. I was overwhelmed by this new dimension I had tapped into. I was no longer caught up between the second and third dimension, but I was truly experiencing the fullness of God. The more I partook of what the Lord was giving, the more I desired to bring forth the vision He had placed in my heart. Even though my leaders had a unique ability to shepherd God's people, I was constantly being drawn into my life's assignment. I was present and faithful, yet disconnected. I went to my new pastor with a cry from within. I knew God was commanding me to be the intercessor He'd sent me back home to be. My pastor released me to go and encouraged me to do everything God had anointed me to do. He also told me that God had revealed to him that I was in transition. During this time, God was commanding me to see myself. Even though my eyes had opened wide to certain things, I still left this last ministry feeling paralyzed. I felt like I needed some person to help me reach my destiny, but the more I reached out to the leaders in the city, the more they pulled away. God allowed this select group of representatives to pull away so I could really see where I was constantly going wrong. I didn't realize I had turned my focus from God to man. I'd left New Living Way Church in hot pursuit for man to help me bring the vision to pass. I knew what God was commanding me to do, but I was allowing man's doctrine to stop me. Instead of stepping out on faith, I found myself joining different ministries, hoping that the pastors would help me walk complete in the call on my life. Sadly, they only had a passion for their own visions. I found myself stuck in a cycle because man kept putting boundaries on the assignment God had given me. My vision was always out of line because it didn't line up with the vision of the house. God was trying to take me to a place in Him where true intercession would be released, and even though God was constantly pushing me to obey, man kept trying to convince me that I wasn't moving according to God's timetable and calendar. There was a command on my spirit; everything within me was letting me know I had entered the "now" season of my life. I stepped out and obeyed the voice of God, and I became the talk of the city. Many leaders scoffed at the fact that no ministry was covering The Anointed Gap Standers Ministries. I couldn't be free to flow the way I knew God was commanding me to flow.

The Lord gave me peace through a dream I had about a young pastor by the name of Jerry Taylor. This pastor changed my view of life, and God used him to uproot man's doctrine from my thinking. I had been told I needed some physical being to release and cover my ministry, but this man of God reassured me that God was my covering and encouraged me to obey God. I felt free for the first time in years. Yes, I was saved, filled with the Spirit of God, yet bound. I couldn't believe how I had allowed the crafty works of the enemy to cause me to sit on my purpose. I

had finally come to the realization that no man is anointed
to do what only God can do.

Acknowledging the Barriers

Therefore then, since we are surrounded by so great a cloud
of witnesses [who have borne testimony to the Truth], let
us strip off and throw aside every encumbrance
(unnecessary weight) and that sin which so readily (deftly
and cleverly) clings to and entangles us and let us run with
patient endurance and steady active persistence the
appointed course of the race that is set before us (Hebrews
12:1 Amp).

The assignment God had given me concerning my city
prepared me for the rest of my life. The things I
encountered throughout the city placed a command on me
to walk in the things of God. As I continued to look
through natural eyes, God's constant momentum was
placed on pause. The truth concerning the leaders caused
bitterness to manifest in my heart. The spirit of bitterness
had enough power to paralyze me. It is of utmost
importance that we always respond to spiritual attacks in
the realm of the spirit. God assigned me to the city to
prepare me for true spiritual warfare. He allowed me to be
confronted with situations that moved me out of the natural,
and once I'd failed to move with God, strongholds began to
grow in my heart. They were barriers that had to be broken

to continue flowing in ministry. I knew God had placed TAGS Ministries within me, but I had to move in the spirit of Christ in every season. There was a lot of brokenness in my heart that demanded attention. I was aware of the God process I had struggled my way through. I was convinced God had used His hand-picked representatives to prepare me for ministry. No one could convince me I hadn't traveled through the process God had ordained for my life. Yes, God had strategically placed men and women of God in my life to point me in the right direction, but while traveling in that direction, I had to remain in the right attitude. God was not going to allow my ministry to reach new levels releasing poisonous venom. I was holding on to hurt and anger, emotions that had manifested a spirit of bitterness in my heart. I knew walking in the fruit of the Spirit had to be my pursuit for me to reach my final destination. Through all my mixed emotions, I've learned that you can only say you are being led by God when His fruit is evident in your life.

God had given me the things I needed to function properly in His perfect will. It was God's will that I release His Spirit through the ministry of intercession, free of distractions. I couldn't let these invisible barriers keep me from reaching my full potential. I had to swallow my pride and repent for moving in the wrong attitude. Once I examined the condition of my heart, I was able to let go and allow God to start the healing process.

Vicious Cycles of Running

So then, brace up and reinvigorate and set right your slackened and weakened and drooping hands and strengthen your feeble and palsied and tottering knees, And cut through and make firm and plain and smooth, straight paths for your feet, [yes, make them safe and upright and happy paths that go in the right direction], so that the lame and halting [limbs] may not be put out of joint, but rather may be cured (Hebrews 12:12-13 Amp).

God allowed me to pray for seven weeks in a local conference room, and I'd left the conference room searching for a place to hold my prayer gatherings. A couple who had just recently moved into the city agreed to allow TAGS Ministries to use their church. Even though their willingness to let me use their church was a kind gesture, my spirit wasn't settled. I've learned that you must be in place in every season of your life so your movements can be synchronized with the move of the Spirit. I was sure God had instructed me to dedicate this season to doing prayer walks, but I was so caught up in the idea of praying within a building. I was also still walking around with bitterness in my heart because of the treatment I had received from different leaders in my city. I had entered a vicious cycle of running because I hadn't released the barriers in my heart.

Once I began praying in the church the couple had agreed to let me use, things began to happen that seemed to squeeze the life out of me, and I was familiar with that suffocating feeling. I can remember experiencing that same pressure when I'd left the last ministry. I felt the way that I felt because I'd joined another ministry instead of remaining focused on the assignment God had given me for the city. I've learned that you can't survive doing things your way. Your agenda must always line up with God's agenda. I had to humble myself enough to hear from heaven. I knew that it was time to do things differently. I had made a trip through the wilderness and it was time for me to go to my very close friends and explain my situation. It was time for me to admit that I had allowed my flesh to lead me. I had to get my life back because I was so tired of running.

I knew it was time for me to get these wrong feelings out of my heart, even if it meant going back to the starting point: my home church. I scheduled a meeting with the leaders who were kind enough to share their ministry with me. The meeting was scheduled for Monday evening. I knew that it was time to get completely delivered from everything that was keeping me bound. I had been fighting truth for months and it was time to turn in my boxing gloves. I was seeking God for words to say to my very

gloves. I was seeking God for words to say to my very
close friends, and God moved through a Word delivered the
Sunday before our scheduled meeting. The preached
message was about the most powerful gift demonstrated
through Jesus and that was love. Through this message, I
found out that I had to release some things from my heart,
and those things were feelings that had continued to destroy
my love walk. It was amazing how God uncovered truth. I
was allowing past situations, misunderstandings, one fight,
and one hurt to hold me captive. It was time I moved
outside of the flesh and into the things of the Spirit. It was
amazing how God used that message to confirm He wanted
me to return to my home church. I knew that I had made
one big circle in the wilderness, but dying there was not an
option. I knew my purpose and I wasn't going to allow
Satan's barriers to keep me from becoming fully developed
in the things of God.

Through my own personal life's experiences, God has
taught me how our emotions can keep us from our
destinies. I can never deny the vicious cycles that took
place in my life, cycles that required fervent warfare
praying. We must put on our spiritual eyes and identify the
enemy in every situation. Once we position ourselves to
receive truth, ungodly cycles and systems are done away
with. God is a God who uncovers and reveals, and He will
never allow us to remain blind to the filth that destroys our

spiritual growth. It is His desire that we prosper and be in good health, even as our souls prosper.

The enemy is crafty when it comes to warping our thinking, but we must take charge over our thought life. *If I could convince her to believe a lie rather than the truth, I gain control.* We must know that this is the way our accuser thinks. He understands the power he can have over us if he infiltrated our minds. This is the reason we are instructed to be transformed by the renewing of our minds. A transformation in the mind takes your eyes off your surroundings and focuses them on your inner most being. A transformation of the mind causes you to see the truth in every situation. We must know that God reveals truth on a powerful level, but we must position ourselves to receive the truth He reveals. We must humble ourselves to apply truth to our lives, and we must know that God's intentions are to deliver us from our own selfish ways.

My Prayer for You

My prayer for you today is that you will always apply truth to your life, and that you will come into the knowledge that it is the truth that sets you free. I pray that your pursuit is always a godly one, allowing God to point you in the direction you should go. I pray that your lifestyle changes atmospheres, never allowing a negative atmosphere to change you. I pray that your walk will always be one of

love and integrity, and that you will truly demonstrate God
to the world and bring deliverance to every bound person
you come into contact with. I pray that God's power will
rest and rule in your life, and the fruit of the Spirit will be
the only thing you release out of your person. I pray that
the truth that dwells in you is not only making you free, but
is also setting free everyone you come into contact with.
In Jesus Name,
Amen.

Chapter 4

Walking in the Nature of the Flesh

For you are still (unspiritual, having the nature) of the flesh under the control of ordinary impulses. For as long as [there are] envying and jealousy and wrangling and factions among you, are you not unspiritual and of the flesh, behaving yourselves after a human standard and like mere (unchanged) men (1 Corinthians 3:3 Amp)?

Throughout this Christian walk, the enemy's ultimate goal has been to keep me out of God's perfect will. I've made many wrong turns, only to end up right back where I started. My life reminds me of the path the Israelites traveled. They walked as blind men in circles, because they allowed the enemy to distract them. God had already given them a promised land, but they had to walk according to His plans and instructions. The Israelites allowed their natural eyes to keep them from the promise. They felt that their end would be death in the wilderness, even though God had promised them life in the Promised Land. Staying focused on God is vital to our walk. We should never allow our environments to take us off God's preordained paths for us. I've turned to man on many occasions, trusting that they would point me in the right direction. I now understand that God is the giver and the deliverer of the vision. I must stay connected to God's plan for my life to receive my abundant life.

Previously, I shared with you how I had to return to the starting point, which was my home church. God wanted to deliver me from responding to my emotions so I could walk with Him, free of distractions. My return to my home church stirred up demonic movement like never before, and I had to respond to every situation in the spirit because I had a devil to fight. The same enemy confronted me upon my return, but this time, the pressure came with more force. I was a minister who desired to serve, but I felt as if my hands were tied. I felt like an eagle with broken wings. My desire to soar was unquenchable, even though I was being held down by an invisible force. The fight was so intense that I wanted out. I knew God had called me to be an intercessor for this local body, so praying was a gift that I couldn't ignore, but I was convinced that I didn't have to remain serving as a minister to fulfill my assignment. God quickly corrected me, and it was a correction I'll never forget.

One Friday morning, I was awakened with a song ringing in my spirit. I heard, "The Potter wants to put you back together again." I heard this song in a way that demanded a response. As I laid in the bed, trying to doze back off to sleep, it seemed as if God turned the volume up a notch or two. The Potter was demanding the clay to move with His movement. I had no other choice but to yield to the move of the Spirit. It was four o'clock in the morning when I pulled myself out of the bed. During this time, I was almost six months pregnant with a belly that looked as if I was nine months pregnant. It wasn't easy responding to the Spirit of God at that time. My flesh wanted to remain in that warm bed, but this attitude didn't move God. He was trying to crucify some things that appeared dead but still had life.

God began speaking Words of wisdom that I continue to hold dear to my heart. I could hear the Lord reminding me to be well balanced (temperate, sober of mind), be vigilant and cautious at all times, for that enemy of mine, the devil, roams around like a lion roaring [in fierce hunger], seeking someone to seize upon and devour (1 Peter 5:8 Amp). The Lord wanted me to maintain a spiritual gaze. He wanted me to be on watch with my guard up. The Lord reminded me of how persistent my enemy was when it came to getting me off the path of righteousness. He didn't want me to lose sight of who I was really fighting. There was nothing natural about the forces that were coming against me, and the only way I could stay watchful and on guard was to remain in the spirit. The devil will never make himself visible to the natural eye; we can only see him roaming in fierce hunger through the eyes of God. So, that enemy of mine was working in the unseen realm, trying to pressure me to respond in the natural. God constantly warned me so that the enemy's weapons wouldn't destroy me. The fight was intensifying because I was getting closer and closer to my promised land.

The journey toward the Promised Land came with a deeper revelation of the power of the flesh. God constantly commanded me to remain in the spirit. He then reminded me of another scripture I love to quote. He directed my attention to the fact that we are not wrestling with flesh and blood [contending only with physical opponents], but against the despotisms, against the powers, against [master spirits who are] the world rulers of this present darkness, against the spirit forces of wickedness in the heavenly (supernatural) sphere (see Ephesians 6:12 Amp). Quoting scriptures is good, but we must allow that Word to produce fruit in our lives. The Word of God must be applied to get the right results.

God has humbled me enough to be transparent so others may be delivered. My experiences as a woman in the pulpit has truly been used to help others. I can remember sitting in the pulpit, feeling cheated and unappreciated. I felt that my gifts were being ignored and I was being attacked by people who should have been building me up. I felt that I had to respond to the attacks with a natural response. I knew that I had to intercede for my church, but I didn't have to do it from the pulpit. I vowed that I wouldn't leave the church in my emotions, but I never mentioned my position as a minister of the Gospel. If my pastor couldn't recognize who I was in the realm of the spirit, sitting with the ministers was a waste of time, but apparently, I had totally forgotten who I was in the realm of the spirit because there was nothing godly about that response. The Lord began ministering to me. He said, "Why respond in the natural if your fight is not coming from the natural?" *I guess you know I felt very sorrowful in my heart.* I had convinced myself that what I was going through had nothing to do with a test, but trust me, this was a test, and I am sure I will forever be tested in this area. I didn't think about the lives I would damage if I stepped down from my position in the spirit. God has called me to be a demonstration of who He is in this earth realm. So I can't embrace the life He demonstrates as an Intercessor and ignore the role He plays as Prophet to His creation. I know that God has given me a voice in this earth realm, and the Inner-Prophet must be released. I refuse to allow my flesh to dominate, and God will continue to have free course in me and through me. I thank the Potter for putting the chipped pieces of my heart back together again.

The things I've suffered as a woman in ministry has truly birthed strength and assurance in me. I know I have walked as a true soldier in the army of the Lord. I have maintained this stand as a soldier so that other women may go through the storms of life knowing that even the worse storm is working together for their good. For years, I felt cheated as a woman in the pulpit, but once I began to view every problem through the eyes of God, deliverance took place in me — I mean complete deliverance.

Maintaining Your Spiritual Gaze

Put away from you false and dishonest speech, and willful and contrary talk put far from you. Let your eyes look right on [with fixed purpose], and let your gaze be straight before you. Consider well the path of your feet, and let all your ways be established and ordered aright. Turn not aside to the right hand or to the left; remove your feet from evil (Proverbs 4:24-27 Amp).

God imparts hope by filling us with vision: a preordained plan, tailor-made just for us. He gives us visions that require we maintain a disciplined spirit. To reach our places of destiny, we must remain focused. I can remember the season God birthed this principle in me. One night after praying, I went to bed and the only light that was shining in the room was a glare from the blinds. The Spirit of God began to show Himself through the glare on the wall. He appeared in the form of the Son of God, Jesus Himself. He began to move up and down and change into different shapes and forms. He then began to speak, "If you keep your eyes on me, you will see me when I move." He proclaimed, "I don't care what happens, stay focused, keep your eyes on me." After that, another vision appeared, but it was a very dark and creepy looking vision. I knew that the enemy had shown up in the room also. This vision of the enemy appeared right over my head, but the Holy Spirit began speaking again, "If you keep your eyes on me, the enemy can't touch you." I stilled my spirit, keeping my eyes only on the vision of Jesus. I maintained my spiritual gaze until the visions vanished and the voice of the Lord had ceased. I was preparing to go to sleep when my youngest daughter, Kimberly, sat straight up in her crib. I jumped off my bed to see if anything was wrong, only to find her sleeping. As I began to lay her back down, the Spirit of God spoke, "Distractions will come, and they are going to come through the ones closest to you." The Lord wanted me to keep a focused mind, no matter what I had to face. This word came directly from the Lord to prepare me for the journey. I knew the enemy would try me. I also knew that my weapon against him was as simple as just staying focused.

It is very important that we live righteous lives, knowing that the unexpected will occur. The enemy is a devil with a plan, and he desires to sift at your strength until you don't have any strength left. I've learned I can love God's ways and God's people and still expect the unexpected. I thank God for the hurt that came directly from the individuals I expected God to use to heal the hurt. God had to teach me not to put confidence in anything or anyone in the natural realm. My job was to remain secure in His power.

I now realize that if I was always cognizant to the devil using anything or anyone, none of his darts would have dazed me. I have learned to trust God and to accept what He allows. I know that I am in Christ, and if I'm in Him, Shelia no longer exists. God is teaching me daily about this flesh of mine that appears to be dead, but rises with power during certain situations. I now understand that it is the unexpected things that God uses to mature us. God has given me a great assignment that I can't walk into lightly, so He has to constantly reveal to me the areas of my life that must be strengthened.

Seeing As God Sees

But the Lord said to Samuel, Look not on his appearance or at the height of his stature, for I have rejected him, For the Lord sees not as man sees, for man looks on the outward appearance, but the Lord looks on the heart (1 Samuel 16:7 Amp).

To maintain a spiritual gaze, you must recognize God's gaze. You must see every situation through the eyes of God. I know I put a lot of emphasis on seeing correctly, but that's because it is very important. Embracing a life of intercession requires excellent vision or sight in the realm of the spirit. The enemy can only present surface matters to you, but God reveals mysteries. It is our job to see truth, regardless of the outer appearance. Our God is not a surface God, and He teaches us to seek the deep things in Him.

Let me share with you a few of my life's experiences that have taught me the importance of seeing through the eyes of God. Before reaching the conclusion of this book, it was booted out of my computer several times. I had typed twelve chapters and my son hit one button and deleted the entire manuscript. In tears, I went to God, asking Him to please show me what I was doing wrong. I was so tired of repeatedly starting over on a book that I knew was destined to make room for me. I came to realize that God wasn't just allowing this to happen, but He was trying to uncover some things to me. I had to allow God to take my book through a spiritual editing. He began to slowly walk me through every chapter, pointing out things that didn't line up with His Word.

False teachings had ended up on many pages of my

book. God wasn't going to allow the enemy to creep into an anointed manuscript. God had placed His hand upon my book, and it was going to be released as a true demonstration of His power. He showed me how man was getting too much glory in the pages of my book. He asked me, "How can a man govern and rule my creation when I am God?" God was letting me know that any time man is exalted into the seat of God, false teachings are being released, either knowingly or unknowingly. He also showed me how the enemy has crept in and established seats in His house. He took my mind back to several books I had read. He began to show me how seeds of false teachings had been planted in my heart through these books. Once this truth was revealed, I was commanded to deal with this situation only in the realm of intercession.

God allowed me to enter into a time of intercession, and during this time of prayer, the crafty ways of the enemy was uncovered on an even deeper level. God showed me how men and women of influence were being used to contaminate God's creation. I was led into what I call rooting out the negative and planting the positive. God was doing surgery on His leaders in the realm of the spirit. The eyes of their understandings were being enlightened, and God alone was receiving the glory.

We must acknowledge God in all things, even in the

books we read. Words are powerful, and they can build up or totally destroy. Throughout my book, God deleted lies and false teachings, reiterating to me that this book would only release the truth about His Word. I had allowed the doctrine of man to creep into my thinking, but, at all times, we must see and release truth. So many people are being drawn away from the Holy Scriptures by different winds of doctrine. We must truly seek to know the Word for ourselves. God is always waiting on us to position ourselves to see things correctly. We should be filled with so much of the Word that we automatically reject false doctrine. We have grown to love books written by men more than the one that was God's breath. Now, don't misread what I'm saying; I'm not against authors because I am one myself, but we must study the Word enough to know when a book is truly inspired by God. I had to begin seeing as God sees to see the truth concerning the information I was putting in my book. I couldn't miss God this time because it was clear to me that my book would never get published if I didn't see correctly. False teachings have crept into the house of God, and as ambassador, I am called to detect and destroy those teachings. To function with this kind of power, I must truly see all things as God sees them. I must also deal with each issue that presents itself in the way God has anointed me to deal with them. I will be held accountable for everything I've done in this body, and it is vital that I respond properly.

I can recall my brother turning to drugs instead of Jesus after losing our mother and sister. During this time, my brother and I lived in different states. Everyone who'd seen him made sure I was aware of what the drugs were doing to him. I hadn't seen him, but my family had painted a mental picture for me. Each time I prayed for him, I could only see the painted image of him in my mind. I cried out to the Lord for his protection, praying that God would keep him safe. Although I'd prayed with much intensity, I still found myself worrying about him. It was very hard to believe for his deliverance. I began taking trips to my hometown to look for my lost and hurting brother, but sadly, God never allowed me to see him. The only thing I had to go on was the image my family continued to paint in my mind.

After traveling home several times and never having the opportunity to see him, I began to question God. I asked Him, "Lord, why won't You allow me to see my brother?" He responded with a question for me: "Who are you looking for?" I released my brother's name as if God didn't know the answer to His question. He replied, "No, you're looking for the painted image in your mind." God commanded me to pray that He reveal the true image of my brother. I had to see him as God saw him. I had been looking for the lie the enemy had shown me. I had to speak life concerning my brother and my prayers were answered. Once I got my gaze right, I began to proclaim that he was saved, sanctified, and filled with the precious gift of the Holy Ghost. I spoke that he was a man after God's own heart. I decreed and declared that he was walking in the commandments of God. I spoke life until all I could see concerning him was life. I no longer saw a broken drug abuser; I saw a powerful man of God, a priest in his house, and an example for his children. Our prayers must become a reality to us before they can manifest in the natural. It was God's will that I view my brother through His eyes. On the surface, he looked a mess, but through the eyes of God, mercy defined him. And through the language of God, words changed him. I am convinced that God desired to release truth on a powerful level. I can proudly say that my brother no longer turns to drugs as his healing agent. Once I was able to see truth, my brother was made free. I spoke life in the spirit until it had no other choice but to manifest in the natural. As long as I maintain my spiritual gaze, I know that my prayers are paving the way for complete deliverance in every area in my brother's life.

I've learned that God is not moved by our intense prayers if we're agreeing with the lies and painted images the enemy presents. We must come to realize how important it is that we see as God sees and deal with matters the way God has anointed us to deal with them. If I would have allowed the imagined image of my brother to remain, the enemy could have taken him out. Lives are depending on us to walk in the spirit. The enemy is not playing games, and he's always waiting on a grand moment to steal, kill, and destroy. It is time for us to wake up because our adversary is not sleeping. He is busy making things happen for his kingdom.

False doctrine has taken on legs and walked into the house of God. A place designed to release the Word of God has been contaminated with the doctrine of man. We have allowed a deceiving demon to take a seat in the midst of the Saints, only because we, as leaders, fail to see correctly. We will be held accountable, and in the end, we will be judged. I've made up my mind to be used by God, regardless of the enemies that will manifest. I have enough sense to know that as long as I remain under the shadow of the Almighty, no foe will overcome me. I know my God-given authority, and because I know it, I will enforce it. It is time that we expose the works of the enemy. The devil has no place in the house of God, and we, as leaders, are commanded to run him out. We are commanded to walk in the spirit, and we must know that this walk means advancement in the realm of warfare. Our spiritual walk can only introduce greater authority to us. It is time to take hold of spiritual matters and remain stable and fixed until we hear God say, "Well done, my good and faithful servants. Well done."

My Prayer for You

It is my prayer that you truly get a revelation of your fleshy nature, and that you will allow God to uncover and reveal truth concerning your emotions. I pray God will give you the ability to see through His eyes, elevating you to truly see the craftiness of our enemy. I pray your natural gaze will be broken and your spiritual gaze will be maintained. I pray the enemy will never gain enough ground to change your view. You will forever see things through the eyes of God, allowing nothing but the Word to penetrate your heart. I pray that the established seats of the enemy are being removed because your eyes are seeing clearly now. I pray that nothing the enemy tries from this day forward will work because your eyes are seeing him. Your hands are taking a hold of him, your feet are crushing him, and your lifestyle alone is utterly destroying him in Jesus name. Amen!

Chapter 5

Dealing with Surface Matters

Sow for yourselves according to righteousness (uprightness and right standing with God); reap according to mercy and loving kindness. Break up your uncultivated ground, for it is time to seek the Lord, to inquire for and of Him, and to require His favor, till He comes and teaches you righteousness and rains His righteous gift of salvation upon you (Hosea 10:12 Amp).

God is seeking leaders who will present surface matters to Him. Every situation that presents itself must be re-presented to the Father. We must take everything to God in prayer. Prayer is the only power that will reconstruct our hearts, giving us the ability to know what Jesus would do in any given situation. Prayer demonstrates a yielding, a spirit of surrender, and a trust that waits on God for instructions.

God used a season of stillness to uncover this truth to me. I saw a lot with my natural eyes, but I wasn't given an opportunity to deal with what I'd seen. I couldn't deal with it in the way I wanted to anyway. The issues that manifested in the church were breathtaking. I had outlined dozens of messages to minister to God's people. I knew I had a lot to say, even though I wasn't given the opportunity to release. One day, during my quiet time, my mind began to revisit situations that needed to be dealt with, and even though I saw a lot, God commanded me to see myself. God asked one question, "Are you ready to address those issues?" I knew the answer had to be no because He only asks questions when I need to examine myself. He began speaking, "The problem that my leaders have today is that they address situations that they're not empowered to address. It is my anointing that destroys the yoke and removes the burden." He then said, "I will not release you to minister until you have first dealt with those issues in the realm of the spirit." I was then reminded of the woman mentioned in the book of St. Luke. She'd suffered with an issue of blood for twelve years. She'd tried everything she could think of in the natural, but found no relief. It wasn't until she touched the supernatural that she received her healing. She had to come into contact with the Great Intercessor, Jesus, and once she touched the anointing, yokes were destroyed in her life. The very issue that came to take her out was completely dried up in the realm of the spirit (see St Luke 8:43-48).

Leaders, God is commanding us to bring everything to Him in prayer. Once we truly activate this principle, giving up on our ministries would be a thing of the past. God showed me how flesh has become the moving force in the church. Words birthed out of pain and not power are being released into the hearts of God's people and He is not pleased. God is waiting on His leaders to truly embrace Him through the power of intercession. We have much preaching in the pulpit but far too little interceding. God moves through words that have been soaked in His presence and released from His very heart. Once we allow the Holy Spirit to deal with our worldly matters, change will manifest. We must cultivate in the realm of the spirit. God is waiting on His heart to be presented to the people. If we would spend more time ushering God's people into His presence and less time screaming into their spirits, change will manifest. A new convert is not truly converted until they meet Jesus. We are led into salvation through confession, but we are led into holiness through the very presence of the holy King. Intercession has taught me the love of the Father. More importantly, intercession has taught me the heart of God. I've learned when to worship, war, or remain still, and I've learned these things through a connection with the very heart of our Creator. Every surface matter originates from the realm of the spirit. It is time we walk out of the natural and into the supernatural. We must present every situation to the Revealer of all things, allowing Him to teach us His love, compassion, and His ability to fight the forces of evil in the unseen realm. It is time to do away with dealing with spiritual matters on the surface. God has given us His Spirit and He expects us to deal with surface matters in the spirit.

Seeing Beyond the Surface

So then, we may no longer be children, tossed [like ships] to and fro between chance gusts of teaching and wavering with every changing wind of doctrine, [the prey of] the cunning and cleverness of unscrupulous men [gamblers engaged] in every shifting form of trickery in inventing errors to mislead (Ephesians 4:14 Amp).

Completing God's assignment for our lives consists of having the ability to see what we're dealing with in the realm of the spirit versus what we see in the natural. Once God revealed to me that I had to bring ministries together through the power of intercession, I had to see what caused the division in the first place. God began to show me the different spirits that were working against His plan for my hometown. Everything came to the surface once The Anointed Gap Standers Ministries manifested in the natural.

Stepping out to start my own ministry was one of the biggest demonstrations of faith I've ever had to make. I was sure God was commanding me to embrace newness. He constantly reminded me that I had to let go of the natural to receive the supernatural. God was letting me know that there was nothing I could do in my own ability. My leaning had to be shifted entirely to Him. I started my ministry by meeting with the intercessors in my living room once a week for a month. I then rented a conference room at one of the hotels in the city. I was certain that God had given me power to come against the territorial strongholds in this area.

During the weeks we'd met in my living room, everyone seemed to be in agreement, but God was revealing to me on a daily basis that the intercessors would fall off. God showed me the spirit that the intercessors were operating in. I thank God that He gives us the ability to see beyond the surface. It wasn't hard to release them because they were not ready for the tasks at hand. The majority of the intercessors who'd shown had come with wrong motives. I was able to detect the spirits of competition, jealousy, and pride. These were the same spirits that were causing the divisions in our city. I knew that there was no way TAGS Ministries could go forth releasing a spirit of division. God was calling us to demolish this spirit, and He was moving obstacles out of the way so my ministry would flourish. I was willing to go through whatever I had to go through to allow God's vision for the city to manifest. God revealed a lot to me during the last meeting I'd held at my house. He'd shown me how forces of evil were working against me. He revealed that the enemy's ultimate goal was to kill my witness, so during this meeting, I explained to the intercessors how important it was that they knew me. I mentioned that lies would be released like never before, and they had to recognize a lie for what it was. A week hadn't passed before several of the intercessors were on the phone, questioning me about rumors they should have known were lies. God told me that I didn't have to waste time defending myself. My job was to obey His instructions, and to do that, I had to remain focused.

February 24, 2007 marked the first service we'd held in the conference room of a local hotel. I stepped out on faith with the determination to do just what God had instructed me to do. He'd revealed to me that I was anointed to gather His people. He began to mark intercessors for the city like never before. He was doing the marking, and I was doing the calling. I called the pastors in the city to tell them the names of the members in their churches who God had marked for intercession, but I could not get any of them to release those intercessors to pray for the city. I knew it wasn't my job to convince them. I obeyed God by letting them know and God had to deal with their hearts.

During this season, I identified a form of godlessness working through many of the local ministries. God began to reveal how the people of God had grown comfortable in seeking the doctrine of man, instead of the true power of God. He also revealed how He would judge us individually. God assured me that we all would be held accountable for the deeds we've done in our bodies. Each one of us is predestined to complete a preordained assignment. We can't become so caught up on the vision of the pastor that we become blind to what God has anointed us to do for His kingdom. Every church I've become a part of had to accept who I was in the realm of the spirit, and if they'd felt like what God had assigned to my life would hinder them, instead of helping them, I had to leave. I can't ignore the role I play in the body because others can't see it. I truly believe that some leaders can't impart the things needed in their church because they're blinded by their own arrogance. They don't have the ability to see when God sends someone in to help bring the vision to pass. Trust me, if God sends a called intercessor into your flock, that person is needed. I know I am anointed to birth God's will into any given situation, and I also know I am a great asset to any ministry God sends me into. God has given me a powerful vision, and I am certain that unity is the only thing that will manifest.

I've learned, as a leader, that I'm anointed to stir up the gifts in others. There are people anointed to make an impact for the kingdom of God, but some leaders are too selfish to see their anointings. They are so caught up in their own agendas that they no longer have the ability to see the things of God. They can only see through the eyes of the flesh. They're working for themselves, all the while, claiming to be working for the kingdom. I know that God has allowed leaders to hurt me instead of helping me so the truth may be told. I've seen some things going on in the church that God is not pleased with. I've seen leaders preaching for their own personal gain, and the people are leaving the house of God in pain. I've seen preachers competing with each other, leaving revivals hoping that they were more powerful than the others who'd preached at that same revival. We can't forget that it is all about winning souls. It is all about presenting Jesus to a lost and dying world. I am certain I am called to detect and demolish things like this that manifest in the church. The season God began dealing with me concerning TAGS Ministries was amazing. I'd received a vision concerning the condition of His Body. The image of His body parts were scattered in different directions. As I released intercession, the ligaments and joints began to connect again. Through this vision, God showed me the power of intercession. He then began saying that He would not freely move in this earth realm until the ligaments and joints of His body come back together again. He explained how a divided body is a dysfunctional body. It is time we realize that Jesus does not have a dysfunctional body. We must see the enemy in the church, and we must deal with him. God said, "My leaders pretended to be blind for so long until they finally became blind when it comes to the things of the spirit. They are letting the enemy choke the life out of the church." God will not dwell in an unclean temple, and it is time the leaders know their roles and walk in them.

God said that intercession is the effective force that will bring the body back together. Intercessors are being raised up to be released to do the work for the kingdom. Preachers, you must know that the four walls of your wooden church is not the kingdom. There are hurting and confused people waiting to be healed, while you are focused on your vision and your vision alone. But in these last days, God is moving in radical ways through the power of networking. We must come together to be considered a body. When we think about a physical body, if the ligaments and joints are disconnected, that body could not stand. This is the same for the body of Christ, and the enemy is totally aware of this.

We become so focused on our own personal visions to the point that we forget why the vision was given to us in the first place. God fills us with vision to benefit His Kingdom. Our individual assignments are like puzzle pieces, and there are many pieces that must come together to complete the puzzle. Additionally, there are many visions that must come together to complete our God given assignments. So, to edify an area that's been broken down, we must build together. The truth must be told because it is the truth that will set us free. Leaders, we must demolish these spirits of jealousy, competition, and pride to edify the body of Christ. The time has come that we see the condition of our hearts and repent.

I couldn't believe the chaos that was stirred when TAGS Ministries manifested in the natural. The manifestation of the vision really brought the truth to the surface. I couldn't get anyone to agree with me concerning this prayer movement for our city. Leaders were too busy to talk with me, and the majority of the people who God marked for intercession were instructed to not participate in intercession by their pastors. I was certain that TAGS Ministries was given to me by God because my finite mind couldn't begin to come up with the strategies that were revealed to me for warfare. I couldn't believe how misled many of the leaders were, but the Bible warns us of false doctrine. False doctrine is anything that doesn't line up with the Holy Scriptures. Everything concerning God's Word is good and pure. The Bible states in Proverbs 4:1-2 (Amp), "Hear, my sons, the instructions of a father, and pay attention in order to gain and to know intelligent discernment, comprehension, and interpretation [of spiritual matters]. For I give you good doctrine [what is to be received], do not forsake my teaching." We have become so comfortable in being fed by men that we're missing the true meat of the Word. The Word instructed us, as individuals, to pay attention to gain and to know intelligent discernment concerning spiritual matters. God is waiting on us to draw directly from His Word, and not from the mouth of man. Our pastors are men and women of God, but they are not God.

We must have a relationship with God to discern whether the truth is coming across in the pulpit. There are too many false apostles, prophets, pastors, and teachers with their own agendas for us not to feast on the Word for ourselves. The Bible lets us know that, "Such men are false apostles [spurious, counterfeits], deceitful workmen, masquerading as apostles (special messengers) of Christ (the Messiah). And it is no wonder, for Satan himself masquerades as an angel of light; so it is not surprising if his servants also masquerade as ministers of righteousness. [But] their end will correspond with their deeds (see 2 Corinthians 11:13-15 Amp). The Bible also states in 2 Peter 2:13 (Amp) , "Also [in those days] there arose false prophets among the people just as there will be false teachers among yourselves, who will subtly and stealthily introduce heretical doctrine (destructive heresies), even denying and disowning the Master Who bought them, bringing upon themselves swift destruction. And many will follow their immoral ways and lascivious doings; because of them the true way will be maligned and defamed. And in their covetousness (lust, greed) they will exploit you with false (cunning) arguments. From of old the sentence [of condemnation] for them has not been idle; their destruction (eternal misery) has not been asleep."

Throughout the Bible, the people of God are warned concerning false doctrine. It is the body of Christ's responsibility to become aware of ungodly people in the church. I've witnessed anointed men and women of God going astray. They are called to work great exploits for the kingdom, but are being held down by men. Colossians 2:18 (Amp) tells us to, "Let no one defraud you by acting as umpire and declaring you unworthy and disqualifying you for the prize, insisting on self-abasement and worship of angels, taking his stand on visions [he claims] he has seen, vainly puffed up by his unspiritual thoughts and fleshy conceit." I've witnessed this going on in God's house, and we must learn to seek God's face for ourselves. God will give us instructions if we would only learn to lean entirely on Him.

I've learned that only God is capable of showing us our destinies. My job as a leader is to always point God's people to Jesus. I do not want the flock of God leaning on and trusting in me to direct them. The Bible lets us know that Jesus is the Way, the Truth, and the Life (see St. John 14:6), so if you want to know the way, seek Jesus! If you want to know the truth, seek Jesus! If you want life flowing in you and through you, seek Jesus! He is the answer to every question.

Exposing False Representatives

Beloved, do not put faith in every spirit, but prove (test) the spirits to discover whether they proceed from God; for many false prophets have gone forth into the world (1 John 4:1 Amp).

Walking through trials and tests becomes easier once you've allowed God's Word to prepare you for the battle. Jesus painted a mental picture of the things I would have to suffer as a true prophet, and He didn't warn me of the unbeliever, instead, He exposed those claiming to be righteous. Jesus proclaims, "O Jerusalem, Jerusalem, murdering the prophets and stoning those who are sent to you! How often would I have gathered your children together as a mother fowl gathers her brood under her wing, and you refused! Behold, your house is forsaken and desolate (abandoned and left destitute of God's help). For I declare to you, you will not see Me again until you say, Blessed (magnified in worship, adored, and exalted) is He Who comes in the name of the Lord!"

I know that every attempt I've made to gather God's people has been unsuccessful for a reason. It wasn't because I didn't come in the name of the Lord. It was because the leaders were too caught up in their own ways of doing things. God knew that the leaders in the city would reject me. He also knew that their rejection would birth a book out of me. I was forewarned about everything I had to face in the city. I'm convinced God's Word is true. If the people of God continue to walk in their own ways, their house will be forsaken and desolate (abandoned and left destitute of God's help) and these Words are from the mouth of the Lord, see St. Matthew 23:37-39 (Amp).

God has shown me the hearts of many leaders in my hometown. He has given me some pretty powerful experiences to ensure I wouldn't walk in the same heart condition. I have seen many striving to make personal accomplishments with their churches because each person wanted to be recognized as having the best church in the city. Instead of unity manifesting, competition and jealousy have been the ruling forces. Their motives for winning souls has only been for personal gain. Instead of Jesus getting the glory that is due to His name, men are taking the praise for themselves.

Leaders are looking forward to their names becoming great amongst men, but for your name to become great in the midst of a people, you must serve the people. Jesus is our ultimate example. He humbled Himself and served the people, even though He was empowered to rule them. St. Matthew 20:25-28 (Amp) states, "And Jesus called the (ten other disciples) and said, you know that the rulers of the Gentiles lord it over them, and their great men hold them in subjection [tyrannizing over them]. Not so shall it be among you; but whoever wishes to be great among you must be your servant, And whoever desires to be first among you must be your slave- Just as the Son of Man came not to be waited on but to serve, and to give His life as a ransom for many [the price paid to set them free]."

As you can see, a true servant's focus is on others and not himself. If we plan to represent Jesus, we must be transformed into slaves of righteousness, and we must deal with the people who are not truly representing Christ. Jesus didn't ignore false representatives, but He exposed them with power. In St. Matthew 21:12-13 the Amplified Bible states that, "Jesus went into the temple (whole temple enclosure) and drove out all who bought and sold in the sacred place, and He turned over the four-footed tables of the money changers and the chairs of those who sold doves. He said to them, the Scripture says, My house shall be called a house of prayer, but you have made it a den of robbers."

As you can see, Jesus dealt with the devil on every level. I know God has elevated a lot of people who can truly see beyond the surface, and they must be given the opportunity to be heard. I know I am one of the many leaders who God has raised up to be His spokesperson, and I will speak the Words that will bring deliverance into the hearts of God's chosen vessels. I've witnessed leaders changing God's holy temple into a den of robbers. I've seen men and women preaching the seed of money instead of the seed of the Word. Leaders, we really don't have to preach money if we're truly preaching the Word. The Word has the power to draw everything needed for the work of the kingdom. If we're truly teaching the Word Jesus taught, men will come. We don't have to water the Word down with our own selfish motives. All we have to do is remain focused on the reason God called us into the kingdom in the first place. We became disciples to make other disciples, and God will supply every need according to the work He has assigned to our lives. Everyone in the kingdom can't receive the same increase because everyone is not called to the same task. There are leaders who God will bless with millions of dollars because of the work that is required by their hands. Even in this, we must remain aware of why He's blessing us on this level. His benefits are given to bring heaven down to earth. Increase, for a leader, does not mean ignore your community and vacation to Florida. It does not mean to take a trip to the mall because you must represent a King by dressing like one. No, your increase was given to win the lost at any cost. It is time that we see our true selves and repent. God will judge us according to the deeds we've done in this body, whether good or bad. God has given us all individual assignments, and when we become focused on obeying Him, God will give us everything needed to accomplish those assignments.

The season I stepped out on faith to start TAGS Ministries was strictly out of obedience. I didn't have any impure motives, and I knew God would provide what I needed for the ministry. There were occasions when no one had shown up for the gatherings, so no offering was given, nevertheless, this didn't shift God's intercession for the city. I trusted He would provide for His own vision. I knew He didn't command me to start a ministry to become a laughingstock to the community. God revealed to me that my trusting Him had to be on point at all times. He wanted my mind to remain on the fact that He is the author and the finisher of my faith. There were times that God didn't allow the money to show up for the conference room until the day before the deadline. God never failed me, and I've never begged or borrowed anything from man. God always moved upon the heart of man to bless me. I know my agenda must be God's agenda at all times. TAGS Ministries is God's vision, and He will forever provide.

I know I've suffered for righteousness sake. I was rejected because I am a true representative of Jesus. In St. Matthew 21:42-43 (Amp), Jesus asked, "Have you never read in the Scriptures: The very stone which the builders rejected and threw away has become the Cornerstone; this is the Lord's doing, and it is marvelous in our eyes." I tell you, for this reason, the kingdom of God will be taken away from you and given to a people who will produce the fruits of it. God has given me a serious assignment, and regardless of the tests I've faced, His assignment for my life remains the same. I know that my attempts at gathering God's people for intercession have been unsuccessful, but I still haven't stop praying. Through my obedience, I have witnessed change. My intercession has been released for a greater reward, a heavenly one. Through my obedience, God has elevated me into new realms of authority, and know that this is a reward that no man can take credit for. Intercession has been released in the secret place, and I have been exalted in the secret place. I know God's assignment for my life will never change. He desires to move through vessels of intercession, and He will continue to raise up leaders until the work is completed. God has anointed me to gather His people, and I know that the intercessory prayer gatherings will manifest. He has given me a special anointing for prayer and intercession, and this cannot be ignored. I know that if I don't bear the burden of intercession, someone else will. So, I refuse to make the same mistakes others have made in the past. The fruit that is ordained to be produced through me shall come forth through the power of intercession in Jesus name.

My Prayer for You

My prayer for you today is that God will give you the ability to see beyond the surface. I pray He will open your eyes to the deep things of Him, and that He will give you the ability to become the eyes and the ears of the church. I pray you will always see every established seat of the enemy, and that you will hear every plot he's creating for your demise. I pray you will embrace your purpose with fixed eyes on Jesus, never allowing the issues of life to cause you to run in the wrong direction. I pray that you will forever examine yourself, keeping your life on the path that leads to your destiny. I pray this chapter has given you a desire to break up your fallow ground, moving you from the realm of the seen into the realm of the unseen, and that you have humbled yourself enough to allow God to teach you how to deal with surface matters in the spirit.

In Jesus Name,

Amen.

Chapter 6

Demolishing the World's Way

Do not love or cherish the world or the things that are in the world. If anyone loves the world, love for the Father is not in him. For all that is in the world--the lust of the flesh [craving for sensual gratification] and the lust of the eyes [greedy longings of the mind] and the pride of life [assurance in one's own resources or in the stability of earthly things]- these do not come from the Father but are from the world [itself] (1 John 2:15-16 Amp).

As leaders for the kingdom of God, there are powerful truths we must release. I've noticed that we often find ourselves pulling away from the principles that will truly edify the church. We find ourselves getting comfortable with just getting by. By this, I mean we live meaningless lives when God has created us to accomplish great things. It is vital that we embrace the truth of God's Word with true manifestations. Jesus is our perfect example, and He expressed His love for us through His sufferings. He cared enough to give up His own will for the will of the Father, and this must become the lifestyle of every believer. The Bible lets us know that it is through Jesus that we have received grace and our apostleship to promote obedience to the faith. The word *obedience* has been a diminishing word in the church. We preach obedience only when we are promoting something for our own personal gain. God is not blind when it comes to the conditions of our hearts. Instead of promoting obedience that leads to discipleship, we promote it only to add to our selfish greed. This has become the state of the church, and we will be judged. If we are to show true spiritual leadership, we must preach from the very heart of God. According to Jeremiah 3:15, we should deliver God's message with knowledge, understanding, and judgment. If we fail to release on this level, we fail to be identified as spiritual shepherds after God's own heart. It is time we examine the condition of our hearts and come into true repentance. This starts with viewing the world correctly. Our view of the world must always be through the eyes of God, and the way we respond to the world must always be God's response. Taking on the role of a leader has nothing to do with us, but everything to do with God. The Bible states, "Whoever says he abides in Him ought [as a personal debt] to walk and conduct himself in the same way in which He walked and conducted Himself" (1 John 2:6 Amp).

As ambassadors of God, we have a work to do for the kingdom, a work that truly demonstrates righteousness, and we must understand that righteousness gives us a distinguishing mark that separates us from the world. The Amplified Bible states in 1 John 1:5-7 that, "This is the message [the message of promise] which we have heard from Him and now are reporting to you: God is Light and there is no darkness in Him at all [no, not in any way]. [So] if we say we are partakers together and enjoy fellowship with Him when we live and move and are walking about in darkness, we are [both] speaking falsely and do not live and practice the Truth [which the Gospel presents]. But if we [really] are living and walking in the Light, we have [true, unbroken] fellowship with one another, and the blood of Jesus Christ His Son cleanses (removes) us from all sin and guilt [keep us cleansed from sin in all its forms and manifestations]."

It is paramount that we recognize the charge God has given us. Change must take place in this earth realm, and it must be released through God's chosen vessels. We are to be true examples of holiness. The world is filled with hurting and confused individuals, people who are seeking for something new and different. They desire change, but can't find it. The place that has been given to us for safety has become a contaminated place. Negativity is found in the place designed to bring hope and restoration, but as a body, and not just any body, but the body of Christ, we are designed to demolish the world's way.

Leaders, we must use our spiritual eyes to recognize the tricks of the enemy. The enemy's craftiness has caused us as leaders to miss heaven, and daily, we are being led away from God's instructions. When we fail to follow all of God's instructions, we abort God's process and take on our own way of doing things. God gives specific instructions when it comes to our destinies. He gives visions that He empowers us to see only through spiritual eyes. The vision is always given to us, but the length of the journey is not. Oftentimes, we'll walk for a long time without seeing the manifestation of God's promises, so consequently, we become discouraged. Once this happens, we begin to go in the opposite direction of God's leading. The enemy comes in and shows us things that are pleasing to the eye. He shows us another way to get to those things, and to the natural eye, his way seems like a quicker and an even better route. But, God's vision for our lives must go through a process before it manifests in the natural. Remember, God is preparing us for ministry. He's rooting out the negative and planting positive things in our lives. This requires patience and endurance, a stillness that is manifested only through focused minds. The Bible encourages us to let endurance and steadfastness and patience have full play and do a thorough work, so that you may be [people] perfectly and fully developed [with no defects], lacking in nothing (James 1:4 Amp). Once patience is perfected in our lives, we can then demonstrate how determined we are to please God. Perfected patience causes us to be faith-standers, people who have a sense of stableness about themselves. A person of faith and patience moves about in radical ways to turn a profit for the kingdom of God. They are not stirred by the pressures of life created by the enemy. They truly understand that there is power in the wait, and they are willing to wait as long as it takes.

It is during the waiting period that the enemy comes in speaking lies. During this time, we should be building ourselves up in our most holy faith, praying in the Holy Ghost. Prayer prepares us for whatever plans the enemy is plotting for our demise. It also keeps our eyes focused on the vision. The minute we lose focus of God's vision for our lives, the truth vanishes and delusions from the devil appear. The enemy will begin to show you an amplified version of how you can get it done quicker, but keep in mind, God is not the author of confusion! He will never use the world's way of doing things to direct you. God is too powerful to lower his standards from holiness to worldliness. His directions will always come through spiritual illumination. Jesus explains in St. John 7:16-17 (Amp) that His revelation is always from His Heavenly Father. He states, "My teaching is not My own, but His Who sent me. If any man desires to do His will (God's pleasure), he will know (have the needed illumination to recognize and can tell for himself) whether the teaching is from God or whether I am speaking from Myself and My own accord and on My own authority."

We are called to be demonstrations of God's power on every level. We can never lose sight of the fact that we were created to represent a King and His name is Jesus. King Jesus has empowered us to defeat the devil on every level. Yes, the enemy will try us: he comes only to steal, kill, and destroy. He desires to steal the dream, kill the passion, and destroy purpose, but even the devil knows that he's not capable of doing this. The question is: *Do we know that he can't do this?* We must keep in mind that we were created to be enforcers. The battle has already been won by Jesus and it is our job to declare the victory. Once we begin to open our mouths to bring forth what the Word says about us, that Word is settled in heaven. Yes, we are born to speak the uncompromising Word of God. We must understand that we are already victorious and it is always our job to continue reminding the enemy of our exalted positions through the shed blood of Christ.

We are empowered to remain fixed in the things of God. The Word has been given as an instrument of power, and God is waiting on us to speak His Word until it overshadows the works of the devil. Our positive confessions kick the devil out of every situation that concerns us. It will take us being steadfast and unmovable when it comes to the things of God to demolish the world's way. For truth to prevail, we must stand on the truth. We must also release the truth of God's Word for our victorious living to be expressed outwardly. The enemy will always show up, but it is our job to deal with Him according to the Word.

It is normal for tests and trials to occur in our lives as Christians. I believe it is all a part of the process, but we must have enough faith in God's Word to sustain us during those trying times. The enemy is the god of this world, and he will always present worldly things to us. It is our job to remain in the spirit, boldly reminding the devil of all the promises given to us through God's Word. The Word is the only thing that can keep us throughout life. It will never change or lose its power, and it is always given to elevate us. The place God desires to take us is spiritual and it is eternal. The devil is always limited, so he can only capture us with natural things. Notice how he tried Jesus, "Again, the devil took Him up on an exceedingly high mountain, and showed Him all the kingdoms of the world and their glory. And he said to Him, 'All these things I will give You if You will fall down and worship me.' Then Jesus said to him, 'Away with you, Satan! For it is written, 'You shall worship the Lord your God, and Him only you shall serve.' Then the devil left Him, and behold, angels came and ministered to Him" (Matthew 4:8-11 KJV).

The Bible tells us that now faith is the substance of things hoped for, the evidence of things not seen (see Hebrews 11:1). I believe that the word now in this scripture describes the kind of faith Jesus used to deal with the enemy in Matthew 4:8-11. I believe that the word now in this scripture places a command on us to move on the devil suddenly. We often allow the devil to talk us out of our belief systems. It is time for us to move promptly into the spirit, demolishing the tactics of the enemy with swift movements of now faith. As you can see, the enemy is limited to presenting to us the world and the world alone, so know that it is his job to keep us operating in the natural realm. We are spiritual beings created in the image of our Spiritual Father, God Himself. It is critical that we embrace the Word of God in the fullness of its power, and condition our hearts and minds to embrace God's perfect will. We should never settle for the limitations of the world. Know that God is presenting eternal things to us, and He's waiting on us to embrace them. The Word is spiritual, and it is our source of power, so it is our job to defend ourselves with the Word of God.

The Power of the Spoken Word
And Jesus answering saith unto them, have faith in God. For verily I say unto you, That whosoever shall say unto

this mountain, Be thou removed and be thou cast into the sea, and shall not doubt in his heart, but shall believe that those things which he saith shall come to pass; he shall have whatsoever he saith (Mark 11:22-23 KJV).

God is a God of promise! He walks us through different stages in life, and regardless of surface matters, He commands us to believe His Word. Throughout the Bible, we are given images of His Word. The Word God speaks is alive and full of power [making it active, operative, energizing, and effective]; it is sharper than any two-edged sword penetrating to the dividing line of the breath of life (soul) and [the immortal] spirit, and of joints and marrow [of the deepest parts of our nature], exposing and sifting and analyzing and judging the very thoughts and purposes of the heart (see Hebrews 4:12 Amp).

We should allow Hebrews 4:12 to brace us in the realm of the spirit. It should root and ground us in a firm and stable foundation. We are taught that nothing can be compared to the Word of God. Regardless of the lies of the enemy, the Word has the power to dominate completely. It weakens the devil's attempts and places us on the winning side.

The Word is always released to perform. It moves into the earth realm proclaiming, "I am God!" The Bible lets us

know that in the beginning [before all times] was the Word
(Christ), and the Word was with God, and the Word was
God, Himself. We are given a command to release the
Word with all the authority and power in Jesus name, and
we must know that the Word has the power to cut away,
purify, convict, counsel, instruct, and defend. It can only
be characterized by energetic work and progressive
movement. I've learned that the Word will be whatever we
need it to be in our lives. It also has the power to do
whatever we need it to do in our lives. It is 100% spiritual
and must be used as our weapon during our times of
warfare. It is very important that we recognize the power
that is in the spoken Word. We live defeated lives only
because we fail to use the power of the Word. We sit idle,
allowing the enemy to destroy our homes, families, cities,
states, and nations. And even though the devil is the god of
this world, we have the power to prevent him from
destroying the world. The devil can only destroy what he's
given the opportunity to destroy. When he finds an
opportune moment, he will rush in to work against the
saints. For this reason, we are reminded to remain vigilant
and cautious at all times.

God sent His only Begotten Son, Jesus, Who is
considered as the Word wrapped in flesh. The devil was
crazy enough to try Him, so who are we? He tried Jesus, so
know that you are not exempt. It is the devil's ultimate goal

to deceive as many as he's allowed to deceive. Saints, it is time we command our spirits to wake up and speak up because the Bible lets us know that every knee must bow at the name of Jesus. We must open our mouths if we plan to win our families, cities, states, nations, and ultimately, the world for Christ. We have to recognize what the Word has already accomplished for us and begin releasing the Word with enough power to see positive results. It is time we use our authority to cut off every attempt of the enemy. We must begin speaking the Word on a level that renders the enemy's tactics ineffective and useless. Now is the time for us to take on a lifestyle of demolishing completely the world's way of doing things!

Snakes Have No Place!

God alone sits in judgment on those who are outside. Drive out that wicked one from among you [expel him from your church] (1Corinthians 5:13 Amp).

I will never forget when God placed a command on me to bring exposure to the snakes in the church. I was back in my hometown, and this time, He had prepared me to do ministry free of distractions. He was letting me know the seriousness of my calling, and He made it clear that it was time out for games. He had given me spiritual eyes to see and anointed my ears to hear. My assignment was to detect and slay the devil, and it was time for me to function according to God's perfect will. I was reminded of a very serious attack I'd endured during my early stage of salvation. During this time, I was wrestling to live a life that was pleasing to the Lord. I had been in a relationship since I was sixteen, and God was bringing complete deliverance into my life. I can remember sharing my situation with a prayer warrior in the church. She laid hands on my stomach, and soon after she'd laid hands on me, demonic spirits entered my bedroom, attempting to rape me nightly. I was literally being violated by invisible enemies. Those spirits held me down nightly with one desire, and that was to penetrate me, but they were never successful in their attempts. I began crying out to God for understanding. I was too embarrassed to share my situation with anyone. Besides, who would believe that I was being violated by demons? Once I started seeking God for clarity, the truth was revealed to me on a powerful level. I had a dream that consisted of me and another sister in the church. We were riding a speeding Ferris wheel, and we were sure the ride would kill us. I looked over at the person controlling the wheel and it was the prayer warrior from the church. Once she realized I'd seen her, the wheel came to a sudden stop. When we stepped off the ride, we were under the control of a demonic spirit. Quickly, I bound the spirit and commanded the attack to cease. Sadly, my friend was still operating under the demonic spirit's control. She began dancing seductively, but as soon as I started casting that demon out of my friend, I was awakened by the phone. No longer asleep, I answered the phone, and on the other line was another sister from the church. She began telling me about a conversation she'd had with the prayer warrior. The caller shared how the prayer warrior had told her about the operation of witches, stating that witches can send incubus spirits out to attack anointed vessels according to the level of anointing that rests upon them. Through the power of the Holy Ghost, the prayer warrior's own tongue was turning against her. She stated that witches can send curses against the purpose that rests upon the individual. She went on to describe the physical conditions that can take place during these satanic attacks. I was experiencing everything that the caller mentioned, and my dream was being validated with every word she spoke. Through this conversation, I received the confirmation I needed to deal with false representatives. I knew God was placing a command on me to bring exposure. Personally, I knew that the prayer warrior was too well-respected to tell anyone about the things she was doing behind the scenes, but she was scattering the sheep with her poisonous venom, and God was not pleased. I have wrestled for years to share this information in my book, but I obeyed after interpreting a dream a minister shared shortly after I returned home. In the dream, the minister was at my house when we noticed something moving under some clothes I had sorted to be washed. We pulled the clothes back, only to find a snake lying on its back and a frog hopping into a pocket on a pair of pants. We then went into my bedroom and found the minister's husband and god child lying in my bed. The minister pulled the covers back and there was another snake lying with his head under the pillow. She pulled the pillow off the snake and it had a human's head. The minister screamed out, "This house is full of snakes! Shelia, let's pray!" The snake, with a weird facial expression, stood up in an attempt to get out of the room, but our prayers caused it to fall against a file cabinet. Once the snake hit the floor, it burst open and released four naked chickens. Now, this is the interpretation of the dream: In the beginning, the minister and I found a snake and a frog under some clothes. According to the Webster's Dictionary, a frog is a stout-bodied amphibian. Webster gave several definitions for a snake, but the best definition for a human headed one read: *a treacherous person; an insidious enemy.*

Both animals were under a sorted pile of clothes. This means it is time for the church to uncover and separate the snakes from the frogs. Notice the word stout described the body of the frog. According to the dictionary, the word stout means: *to be courageous; brave: stout warriors.* We have some stout warriors who need exposure to advance in the kingdom of God. God is commanding his stout warriors to come out of hiding, so the treacherous, insidious enemies can be dealt with. Notice in the dream that the stout soldier had the enemy on his back. At first glance, the frog appears fearful because he was hopping into a pocket, but one of the definitions Webster's Dictionary gave for the word pocket is to *endure without protest, to conceal or suppress.*

To suppress, according to Dictionary.com, means to put an end to the activities of, to do away with by or as if by authority, abolish, stop. God is placing a command on His stout warriors to put an end to the works of the devil.

The dream takes us into another room, where we find a human headed snake in the midst of loved ones. God is saying that the snakes are sitting among the congregation of Saints. They are comfortable in their positions, while the enemy uses them to bring harm to our loved ones. It is time we stand up in the authority God has given us. He has given us the power to stand as brave and courageous soldiers in the house of the Lord. Once we begin to operate according to the Word of God, exposure will automatically be brought to the insidious enemies in our midst.

Once the minister and I began operating in the realm of spiritual warfare, the snake fell and released everything it had consumed. The end of the dream really blessed me because the snake had devoured the fearful ones. He was full of chickens that were naked with no covering. This signifies that the enemy will always go after people who lack substance. The Word is our substance, and when we fail to walk as true representatives of God, we are bound to be devoured by the enemy.

I have been truthful concerning my attacks in the house of God, and through my obedience, God has given me peace through His Word. My reward is found in Psalms 64 (Amp). It reads, "Hear my voice, O God, in my complaint; guard and preserve my life from the terror of the enemy. Hide me from the secret counsel and conspiracy of the ungodly, from the scheming of evildoers, who whet their tongues like a sword, who aim venomous words like arrows, who shoot from ambush at the blameless man; suddenly do they shoot at him, without self-reproach or fear. They encourage themselves in an evil purpose, they talk of laying snares secretly; they say, Who will discover us? They think out acts of injustice and say, We have accomplished a well-devised thing! For the inward thought of each one [is unsearchable] and his heart is deep. But God will shoot an unexpected arrow at them; and suddenly shall they be wounded. And they will be made to stumble, their own tongues turning against them; all who gaze upon them will shake their heads and flee away. And all men shall [reverently] fear and be in awe; and they will declare the work of God, for they will wisely consider and acknowledge that it is His doing. The [uncompromisingly] righteous shall be glad in the Lord and shall trust and take refuge in Him; and all the upright in heart shall glory and offer praise."

The time has come that God Himself is dealing with the people proclaiming to be righteous. He is not blind when it comes to the things that present themselves in His house. Snakes have crept into the house of God, and because the world's thinking has crept into the minds of our leaders, sin has established a seat. Sin is resting in the church from the pulpit to the back door. We can't see holiness because the secular is taking over the sacred. We must be real with ourselves and ask how secularism has become the state of the house of God. Is it because the impure spirits of selfish ambition and greed have caused sin to elevate in the church? Could it be that the desire for the fastest growing church has caused our leaders to be blind, thereby aborting the purpose of the vision? If any of this is true for your church, know that you have your reward, and in the end, you will be judged. Ezekiel 22:25-28 (Amp) states, "There is a conspiracy of [Israel's false] prophets in the midst of her, like roaring lion tearing the prey; they have devoured human lives, they have taken [in their greed] treasure and precious things; they have made many widows in the midst of her. Her priest has done violence to My law and have profaned My holy things. They have made no distinction between the sacred and the secular, neither have they taught people the difference between the unclean and clean and have hid their eyes from My Sabbaths, and I am profaned among them. Her princes in the midst of her are like wolves rending and devouring the prey, shedding blood and destroying lives to get dishonest gain. And her prophets have daubed them over with whitewash, seeing false visions and divining lies to them saying, Thus says the Lord God - when the Lord has not spoken."

Know that God is moving in this season in radical ways. He is demolishing the world's way, and He is rooting out the negative. His Word is being planted into the minds of believers on another level. The apostle, prophet, evangelist, pastor, and teacher are taking their rightful places in the kingdom. No longer will the enemy delude their minds with false images of wealth and riches. The body of Christ is becoming a perfected one. Saints are being presented as consecrated people of God, holy temples who demonstrate oneness in the faith. God's commanding a spirit of humility to take precedence in our lives. Through our yielded hearts and willing spirits, reconstruction is taking place. A tearing down and a rebuilding of the temple is taking place in the realm of the spirit. Pride is being cast down like lightning, and the true light of the Gospel is being presented. The spirit of competition and jealousy holds no position in the kingdom of God. Everything that is good, pure, and holy is being released into the earth realm. The believer and unbeliever alike are making their way to the altar. Human hearts are being washed as white as snow, demolishing every symptom of darkness. We are living in an hour of change, a level of change that is presented for every eye to see.

God has placed a command on our spirits to truly demonstrate love. Deliverance is running its course and God alone receives the glory. The kingdom of God suffered violence, but the violent take it by force. God is establishing His kingdom and the devil does not have enough power to stop Him!

My Prayer for You

My prayer for you today is that you take on a lifestyle of demolishing the world's way of doing things. I pray you will embrace a lifestyle of demonstrating the true light. God has given you a special ability to give off a radiating light. I pray that through your release, many will come to Jesus with the desire to live holy. God is not slack when it comes to His people, and I pray you will always know that He is a present God in your life. He is a God who takes pleasure in blessing His people. Know that God is not slack concerning His promises when it comes to you, and know that He continues to impart power to you to deal with the enemy. I pray you will embrace the power He has given you through His Word, and I also pray that you will release the words that will expose and demolish every seat of Satan that is hidden. It is my desire that you become the warrior God has created you to be. God is waiting on you to make the enemy very uncomfortable, and He is waiting on you to make it impossible for Satan to sit comfortably in the midst of the congregation. I pray you never sit idle, allowing the enemy to destroy your life, and God will give you a level of boldness to destroy the spirit of carnality on another level. Know that wickedness is being driven out of the church with power, and you are one of the many enforcers God is using to drive it out.

In Jesus Name,

Amen.

Chapter 7

Taking Inventory of Yourself

Do not judge and criticize and condemn others so that you may not be judged and criticized and condemned yourselves. For just as you judge and criticize and condemn others, you will be judged and criticize and condemned, and in accordance with the measure you [use to] deal out to others, it will be dealt out again to you. Why do you stare from without at the very small particle that is in your brother's eye but do not become aware of and consider the beam of timber that is in your own eye! Or how can you say to your brother, Let me get the tiny particle out of your eye, when there is the beam of timber in your own eye? You hypocrite, first get the beam of timber out of your own eye, and then you will see clearly to take the tiny particle out of your brother's eye (St. Matthew 7:1-5 Amp).

I was inspired to write this chapter after God revealed some deep-seated issues in my life. I had walked with God for years and had never realized the things that needed to be purified in my life. I thought I had it all together, but everyone around me needed some serious help. After years of correction, I now understand that change starts with self-evaluation. I know that you can't truly see until you're able to see the filth that is in your own life. You must learn to examine your own heart before you can begin to evaluate someone else's.

Once we know that we have a call on our lives, we should never lose focus of what matters the most. God has empowered us to witness, and we shouldn't allow anything to damage our character. Daily, we should examine ourselves and not those around us. We cannot grow in this walk with God ignoring truth. The Lord will forever show us ourselves, but we must remain humble to receive the truth He reveals. It takes staying in the right state of mind to see the darkness that is active in our own lives. The season God instructed me to return to a particular ministry was a season of a self-evaluation. I had been pointing out the wrong in my leaders for a whole year. I couldn't see myself for examining them. God began to instruct me to cut certain people off. There were people in my life who were releasing nothing but negative words. Once I obeyed God in cutting them off, I was able to see myself. The Lord began to show me how I had allowed the devil to change my view of my leaders. I was instructed to return to my home church on a Wednesday night. On this particular night, the leaders were out of town. This gave God enough time to really show me my own heart. The following week, I was able to meet with them and God instructed me to only talk about my own flaws. I was not allowed to point out the wrong in them. It was my job to examine myself and return to serving under them with a humble spirit.

This experience taught me how to tally my own personality traits, aptitudes, attitudes, skills, and shortcomings. If we fail to take the time to do a self-evaluation, we will never be qualified to give wise counsel. We sit back waiting on God to change situations and circumstances, but God is trying to change us. He is trying to show us ourselves on a daily basis. We can pray strong prayers of petitions, abstain from certain meals, tarry in shut-ins, and still end up more drained and bound than we were before. This takes place in the lives of saints only because we refuse to see our own shortcomings. We must come to realize that even though we are saved, we still need to be delivered from our old ways of thinking.

Taking inventory of ourselves allows us to see our innermost being, and gives us the chance to grow in this walk with God. I can vividly recall God leading me into a twenty-one day fast. I went into the fast strongly expecting God to give me instructions on how to deal with the people surrounding me. After obeying God, I began to elevate in the things of the Spirit. I was exalted only because I allowed Him to show me myself. I was dealing with things I saw active in others, and I wanted God to manifest change in them. I was good at seeing the heart conditions of others, but God was conditioning me to see my own heart. He uncovered things that left me speechless. He asked me questions that caused me to see all the bitterness I had in my heart, and this bitterness was directed at His creation. The truth of the matter was, I needed help and God began to show me how much I needed to embrace the things of Him. The questions allowed me to see how far off focus I had become.

We can spend our lives focusing on the negative to the point that we're completely blind to the positive. Growing in this life with Christ consists of seeing everything through the eyes of God and that includes seeing the truth about yourself. We have to allow God to take us through a process of taking out the filth of the flesh and building us up in the things of Him.

God used fasting as one of the refining processes to reveal to me what I really looked like through His eyes. The fast caused me to be sensitive to the voice of God. I now know that the crucifixion of my flesh caused my spirit to be more receptive to the truth. Everything that was taking residence in my heart that was not of God was exposed. God began to cleanse me from everything that was sent to hinder my walk with Him. I entered the fast sure that I had it all together, but everyone around me needed some serious help, but, as you can see, the problem was hidden under the filthiness of my flesh. The problem wasn't other people at all; the problem started with me. I was taking inventory of others and losing focus on what my life consisted of. Once we begin to feel like we're so good that we can point fingers at others, it is time to take inventory of ourselves. Let us not make going to church, reading our Word and praying so routine that no change takes place in our inner man. We are to give ourselves to the things of God so change can manifest in our hearts.

Within a week's time on the fast, God had revealed to me that I was walking in the wrong spirit, and He was not pleased. He led me to Colossians 3:8-17 (Amp). It states, "But now ye also put off all these; anger, wrath, malice, blasphemy, filthy communication out of your mouth. Lie not one to another, seeing that ye have put off the old man with his deeds; And have put on the new man, which is renewed in knowledge after the image of him that created him: Where there is neither Greek nor Jew, circumcision nor un-circumcision, Barbarian, Scythian, bond nor free: but Christ is all, and in all. Put on therefore, as the elect of God, holy and beloved, bowels of mercies, kindness, humbleness of mind, meekness, longsuffering; Forbearing one another, and forgiving one another, if any man have a quarrel against any: even as Christ forgave you, so also do ye. And let the peace of God rule in your hearts, to which also ye are called in one body; and be ye thankful. Let the word of Christ dwell in you richly in all wisdom; teaching and admonishing one another in psalms and hymns and spiritual songs, singing with grace in your hearts to the Lord. And whatsoever ye do in word or deed, do all in the name of the Lord Jesus, giving thanks to God and the Father by Him."

As you can see, all of my ill feelings had to go. For God to elevate me in the things of the Spirit, I had to take off anger, rage, and bad feelings and replace them with bowels of mercy, kindness, humbleness of mind, meekness, and longsuffering. Saints, this is all Jesus had to maintain to walk in purpose, and we are called to represent Him.

Releasing the Real You

I have been crucified with Christ [in Him I have shared His crucifixion]; it is no longer I who live, but Christ (the Messiah) lives in me; and the life I now live in the body I live by faith in (by adherence to and reliance on and complete trust in) the Son of God, Who loved me and gave Himself up for me (Galatians 2:20 Amp)

I have learned through experience that you can't really see yourself until you look within yourself. The real person

God has created you to be is down on the inside waiting to come out. Once God had me to take inventory of myself, I began to really look within. I realized that the real Shelia was smothered, buried under the issues of life. I also realized that I had come to a point in my life where the real me was screaming to come out. I had reached a season where the only thing that mattered was God's will for my life. I realized that I had made some wrong turns in my life and ended up on dead end streets, only because I didn't seek guidance from my heavenly Father. I knew I'd made some major decisions without involving God, and I was reaping the consequences of my actions.

I have come to realize that flesh can really mislead a person, and we should never get caught up in the rudiments of the flesh. We should, at all times, remind ourselves of how fully developed we are in Christ. We no longer have to give ourselves to the leading of the flesh; we are now free to serve God in complete dependence upon His Person. I couldn't see how I was allowing my flesh to lead me down wrong roads until I began to take inventory of myself.

I used to base my life on what my natural man wanted, but now, it is all about the real me. When a true examination takes place, you will begin asking yourself some serious questions. I asked myself, "What does the real Shelia want for the rest of her life?" I now desire that my life be surrounded with the things of God. I want everything I do to bring glory to God. I now realize that I'll never see the fullness of God if I continue giving my attention to the things of the flesh. Being led by the flesh, I married in a season that I wasn't prepared mentally or spiritually. I found myself living a life caring about nothing but keeping a smile on my husband's face. I couldn't allow the real Shelia to come out because I knew everything around me would change. My total focus was on keeping him happy, even if it meant not walking complete in Christ. The fear of losing my husband had a strong hold on me. I would ask myself questions like, "If I allow the real Shelia to come out, will my husband still feel comfortable with me? If I allow the witness to come out, will he still love me? If I share half of the things with him that I desire to share, will he still look forward to coming home to me? If I share with him what I really want in a husband, will he still embrace me with a loving kiss?" These questions had made my heart their home. I had allowed fear to rob me of being complete in Christ. I thought I loved my husband with every fiber of my being, but the truth of the matter was, I didn't completely love him.

The Bible teaches us, in 1 John 4:18 (Amp), that there is no fear in love [dread does not exist], but full-grown (complete, perfect) love turns fear out of doors and expels every trace of terror! For fear brings with it the thought of punishment, and [so] he who is afraid has not reached the full maturity of love [is not yet grown unto loves complete perfection]. Because the enemy knows that fear works against our completeness in Christ, he uses it as one of his strongest weapons. The Bible also tells us to know that who the Son sets free is free indeed (see St. John 8:36). Are you really free when you desire to minister, but are afraid of what the outcome may be? Are you really free when you need to talk, but are afraid you won't capture the attention of your spouse? Are you really free when you long to sit and enjoy deep conversations with your spouse, but are afraid you may be a little too deep for your spouse? I had developed many questions over the years, and stored them up in my heart-questions that needed answers.

Allowing your real spiritual side to come out shouldn't be based upon how someone else feels. We have to come into contact with who God created us to be before we can attempt to please someone else. After I really began to look within myself, I realized I had to deal with my issues immediately. I knew I had to reveal my real side to my husband before I could bring anything into my relationship with him. I came to the conclusion that I could not live out my entire life never experiencing the fullness of God because I had allowed the issues in life to bury me. I knew if I didn't open up, I'd die never knowing how it felt to express my deepest and most intimate thoughts. I'd live out my life settling for less when God has empowered me to embrace the very best. Every moment I wasted not dealing with this problem was another day trapped and smothered, but being afraid to do or say anything is not a part of God's will for my life. I now know that fear has nothing to do with the liberty of God. The Bible informs us that God hath not given us the spirit of fear; but of power and love and a sound mind (see 2 Timothy 1:7).

Taking inventory of my life has allowed me to see what lies dormant on the inside of my heart. I have come to the conclusion that it is a must that I walk complete in Christ. I know I can't live out my life holding back what's on the inside of me. I understand that the very thing I'm afraid to allow to come out is the very thing that will bring power. If we allow fear to prevail, there is no way of tapping into the power God has freely given us.

You are Uniquely Designed

But seek (aim at and strive after) first of all His kingdom and His righteousness (His way of doing and being right), and then all these things taken together will be given you besides (Matthew 6:33 Amp).

We enter into this world taking on the ways of our

environment. Our surroundings instruct us, the people around us conform us, and the steps of another direct us. Our preordained path is hidden by our natural surroundings. We find ourselves forever seeking fulfillment in a limited world. When we fail to see beyond the natural, we fail to truly live. We must understand that God's kind intentions can only be found in His presence. And regardless of the wonderful plans God has for us, we can't embrace them until we have the ability to see them.

Once we enter into the presence of God, hope comes on the scene with a sighing relief, a sense of comfort that lets us know that life was intended to run a little smoother. For years, we find ourselves holding on to things that will never fit into God's preordained plan for our lives. Our lives were written out before the foundation of the world, and God created us according to His divine purpose.

We grew up creating our destinies through the accomplishments of others. Families seek housing in particular communities because of the people who make up those areas. Leaders start churches and lead those churches according to the vision and leadership of other leaders. We fail to seek the Creator for our own special blueprint. We were all created with a unique design. Apostle Paul explains it this way in 1 Corinthians 12:4 (Amp), "Now there are distinctive varieties and distributions of endowments (gifts, extraordinary powers distinguishing certain Christians, due to the power of divine grace operating in their souls by the Holy Spirit) and they vary, but the [Holy] Spirit remains the same. The Word is encouraging us to find out who we are according to God and not man."

I have found myself going in circles because I yielded to the guidance of the flesh. My unique design for ministry had remained buried under the issues of life because I responded to the ways and purposes of the world. I now know I can only enjoy my abundant life walking in my true identity. I also know that an exchange must take place to demonstrate who God called me to be.

I can remember having a talk with one of my closest friends, and I wasn't asking any questions, neither was I waiting for answers. I knew the answers and was fully capable of solving my dilemma. I was in a stagnated place where there was no constant flow in my life naturally or spiritually. My hands were tied and my dreams were placed on pause. Now, this was my situation because I chose to hold on to things that needed to be disregarded in my life. The truth was crying out and my better life was depending on me to respond properly. I shared things with my friend that changed everything about my thinking.

Renovation was taking place in my mind and something stronger and more lasting was being constructed. My better had been placed on hold for all the wrong reasons. I had been edifying everything around me except the things that mattered the most. My real spiritual self had been placed in a holding place so others could be built up. That's the life of an intercessor. We are called and appointed to stand in the gap on the behalf of others. We've been given power to go between the problem and the answer and risk our lives for our brethren. I must admit that the assignment I was taking on had nothing to do with the things of the spirit.

For years, I had taken off my true spiritual identity. I had stepped out of my true self to gratify things that had nothing to do with the kingdom of God. Now, don't get me wrong, no one tied my hands and made me do this. All of this came about because I chose to put other people's needs before mine. These actions were very familiar and the only thing this familiar place delivered was pain. I ignored who I was designed to be so I could bring joy to others. As I continued to please man, I quickly got away from demonstrating the woman of God I was called to be. This conversation with my friend became the light that guided me. The more I talked with her, the more I was commanded to demolish this roller coaster lifestyle. I was living an up and down life, not because I wasn't aware of the direction I should have been taking, but because I constantly returned to the life that pleased man rather than God.

It is our Savior's desire that we are sanctified and holy. In St. John 17:16-19 (Amp), the Lord states, "They are not of the world (worldly, belonging to the world), [just] as I am not of the world. Sanctify them [purify, consecrate, separate them for Yourself, make them holy] by the Truth. Your Word is Truth. Just as You sent Me into the world, I also have sent them into the world. And so for their sake and on their behalf I sanctify (dedicate, consecrate) Myself, that they also may be sanctified (dedicated, consecrated, made holy) in the Truth"

I've written and rewritten things in this book only to uncover the truth. I've learned that the truth will stand when everything else is destroyed. Once God places you in a position as an ambassador for the kingdom, He shines His radiating light into everything you're connected to. God has a way of disturbing our lives when it does not line up with His perfect will. When our associations confuse the plans of God, a disconnection must take place. Staying true to who God created us to be must become more important than anything else in this world.

My Prayer for You

It is my prayer that you will see the truth about yourself,

and that you will position yourself to go through the purifying process. God is waiting on the opportune moment to create in you the heart you'll need to secure a great future for yourself. I pray every decision you make will be based on the love of God and not the fear of the enemy. It is my prayer that you will tap into the power God has freely given you and that you will never allow your surroundings to cause you to ignore the power within you. I pray you will never allow fear to be the dominating force in your life, and that you will always embrace the power, love, and the soundness of mind God has given you. I pray that you will always take inventory of yourself because this will lead you into all truth. I pray, in Jesus name, that nothing God has given you will lay dormant within you. I also pray that you will never grow content until you begin to release the real you, and that you will never allow anything to distract you from doing what you were created to do. I speak into your life the boldness and the momentum you'll need to get to your destiny, and I rebuke even the thought of giving up.

In Jesus Name,

Amen.

Chapter 8

Knowing Your Purpose

I therefore, the prisoner for the Lord, appeal to and beg you to walk (lead a life) worthy of the [divine] calling to which you have been called [with behavior that is a credit to the summons to God's service (Ephesians 4:1 Amp).

We have to be confident of this one thing: that He Who has begun a good work in us will continue until the coming of Christ (Philippians 1:6). Over the years, I've learned how important it is that you know who you are in God and the area of ministry He has called you into. Everyone is not going to understand the ministry God has placed on the inside of you, and that's okay, just as long as you walk worthy of the vocation wherewith you've been called. The enemy will always do his job to get you to take your eyes off God. I can recall a woman coming up to me one Sunday evening at church. She'd said to me, in so many words, that I couldn't discern between good and evil. She was convinced that I couldn't discern between God using me and the devil using me. Now, why would I allow her opinion to tell me where I was spiritually? She was convinced that I was allowing the enemy to use me, and she'd gotten really upset when I wouldn't agree with her. Because, I know to guard my heart and the anointing that God has placed on my life, I instantly put up a defense that wouldn't be moved. I rebuked every negative seed that was trying to take root in my spirit. First of all, I know I've been empowered to know the enemy and his tactics. I've also been empowered to come against his tactics. I know my place, and I know that God expects me to stand up against anything the enemy tries to send my way.

The Bible teaches us that the weapons of our warfare are not carnal but mighty through God. It goes on to tell us to cast down imaginations and every high thing that exalts itself against the knowledge of God and to bring into captivity every thought to the obedience of Christ (2 Corinthians 10: 4-5 KJV). It is vital that we deal with words released to hinder our progress in the Kingdom. I immediately recognized the enemy and began to capture every negative seed before it took root in my spirit. I couldn't deal with the situation as if it were the individual trying to get me off focus because the Bible teaches us, in Ephesians 6:12, that we are not contending with physical opponents. Even though I saw the enemy, and I stood up against all his plans, I still had to speak life to myself. I had to tell myself that I know who I am in Christ. I know that I am the righteousness of God in Christ Jesus. I had to tell myself that greater is He who lives in me than he who is in the world. I'm convinced that I'm saved, sanctified, and filled with the wisdom of God, and nothing by any means shall harm me. The Word of God is my defense, and when everything else fails, the Word will stand. The enemy will come in, and sometimes, he will come in like a flood, but the Word of God will lift up a standard against him. It is important that we believe the Word because the Word alone is our defense.

God has given us everything required to live a righteous life. He has called us out of darkness by an effective and eternal force, a force that can't be compared to any other power in this universe. The same power that called us out of darkness is the very power that dwells on the inside of us. We are now marked with the power and ability to act with strength, with might, and with force. Jesus promised us this power in Acts 1:8 (Amp). He states, "But you shall receive power (ability, efficiency, and might) when the Holy Spirit has come upon you, and you shall be My witnesses in Jerusalem and all Judea and Samaria and to the end (very bounds) of the earth. God has presented unto us His gift of love and we have no reason to fall short of His glory. For He foreordained us (destined us, planned in love for us) to be adopted (revealed) as His own children through Jesus Christ in accordance with the purpose of His will [because it pleased Him and was His kind intent]-[So that we might be] to the praise and the commendation of His glorious grace (favor and mercy), which He so freely bestowed on us in the Beloved. In Him we have redemption (deliverance and salvation), through His blood, the remission (forgiveness) of our offenses (shortcomings and trespasses), in accordance with the riches and the generosity of His gracious favor" (see Ephesians 1:5-7 Amp).

Once we made the decision to ask the Spirit of God to live in our hearts, we agreed to represent Him in the authority of His power. We are obligated to show forth the power that has been vested in us at all times. God is now calling His church to a life of intercession, and this requires becoming destructive in the spirit. To truly enforce the cross of victory, we must fight. Yes, we must do true spiritual warfare to maintain a life of pleasing our heavenly Father.

Embracing this life as an intercessor came with serious warfare. I've had to walk through many storms to know who I am in the realm of the spirit. I've faced difficulties on every level, yet and still, I have embraced the fullness of the call on my life. I wasn't able to see my exalted position until obedience prevailed. Regardless of what I was seeing with my natural eyes, I had to obey the voice of God. God anointed me to release intercession in my city and I obeyed Him, regardless of the unseen forces that came against me.

The only thing I could hear the Spirit of God speaking into my spirit was diligence. I knew I had to remain persistent in and out of season. There were many obstacles in my way, but I knew I had to stay true to the vision. God empowered me to release change in the city through the power of intercession. As I obeyed God, the assignment became clearer to me. God was about to do something supernatural, and it was too powerful for the natural realm to comprehend. Natural eyes couldn't began to grasp the accomplishments that was about to be made in the spirit.

My diligence had to be on point in this season, and the vision became clearer once I obeyed in the small things. The attacks came from every direction, even from the people I thought would help me, but God was building me up on the principle of diligence. I remained focused, regardless of what the enemy was using against me. Faithfully, TAGS Ministries obeyed God, and we were astonished when we began to see the manifestations of our intercession. The experiences we had during the seven weeks God instructed us to pray in the conference room were amazing. We didn't give up, even though most of the intercessors God marked for prayer at that time didn't show up. We knew God was pleased with our obedience. He moved through our intercession in ways we couldn't believe. The first service was held February 24, 2007, and I can truly say with boldness that the Spirit of God moved with power. My spiritual mother and I went in an hour early so the Spirit of God could set the atmosphere. I was led to pray over the chairs in the first and second row only. God really released His power into one particular chair. I was then instructed to place a note under this chair. It stated, "There is a healing in the house for you." Before dismissing the prayer service, I was led to ask the individual sitting in the chair to read the note. She received the Word and testified, saying she knew that it had to be God. She even went as far as to share the issue she was battling with. This really amazed everyone in attendance, including me. This was truly a God move! There was no way I could have known that this chair would be occupied. We learned during our very first service that lives were depending on us to be obedient to the voice of God.

On March 3, 2007, we had a decent-sized group of intercessors during service. The praise and worship music played as we reverenced God's presence. His Spirit swept through the service like gigantic waves. My spiritual mother began to run gracefully around the room with one finger up and the other hand was lifted in praise. It appeared as if she was saying, "Excuse me, but I have to praise Him!" As she moved with God's movement, a shift took place in the atmosphere. Every person who understood the manifestation of intercession moved with God. We were all travailing in the spirit as described in

Romans 8:28. God truly moved through our intercession during this particular service, and we knew that true accomplishments were being made in our city.

My spiritual mother was the trailblazer for the move of the Spirit during this service. She began weeping excessively, weeping that came from so deep within that it could be felt. Mother then began to cry out, "There's a sound that the intercessors must hear, God is releasing a sound!" By this time, I was standing to my feet and wailing as if there was a trumpet in the room. The sound of a horn took over my body and it was so intense that I fell to the floor shaking under the power of God. The power that was released in this small conference room was unbelievable. We knew that regardless of the contrary hearts in our city, God had placed a command on the intercessors to pick us up in the realm of the spirit.

March 10, 2007 marked TAGS Ministries' third gathering. This meeting was totally different from the other two. My spiritual mother and I were the only intercessors who showed up. When we walked into the conference room, we found the chairs set up totally different from the way we'd asked they be organized, but instead of giving energy to the devil, Mother and I began to rearrange the chairs. The enemy meant this for bad, but God used it to teach us intercession on another level. As we moved the chairs, we tapped into the power of seeing beyond the surface. God wanted our focus to be on the chairs during this service. We had to move each chair on the end of every row. God wanted us to make a complete circle around the chairs, and as He gave the instructions, we obeyed. After moving the chairs, I was led to lay the city's map on the altar. We began to lay hands on the map and our weeping came from so deep within our hearts. God was using human hearts to birth His will for our city. We wept over the city for what seemed like hours, and after we'd shed tears for our city, we were led to anoint the map with holy oil. We remained sensitive to the Spirit because there were certain streets that really concerned God.

Once the map was placed on the altar, the Lord revealed to us that the chairs had become the city. On the top right side of the map, the name of our city was printed in large letters. We had to place a chair in the same position in the conference room. The Spirit of God flooded my spirit with strategic instructions. We were to walk around the city and speak life. As the Spirit of God moved upon us, we were to lay hands on the chair that symbolized the whole city, and decree and declare His Word over it. We obeyed the Spirit of God, and each time a decree came forth, it was strong and forceful. God was really demolishing the works of the devil in our city. We walked, laid hands on the chair, and decreed until God gave us more instructions. We found ourselves back on the altar standing over the map. God was not finished using us to intercede for our city. He began to have us pray over different chairs in the conference room. They were symbolic of the various streets in the city. We had to be open to the Holy Spirit's direction because He would give us the streets that were on His agenda for the day. Immediately, my spiritual mother started laying hands on the chairs. God began to reveal streets and the territorial strongholds that governed those particular areas. He also revealed the two establishments that the devil was using to bind His people. I was amazed at the level of intercession God was tapping us into. Mother began to literally see the buildings because God was tapping her in and out of visions. He began to uncover every high place that our intercession was tearing down. The works of the devil were being demolished through two yielded vessels.

March 17, 2007 marked the fourth intercessory prayer service. An assigned group of intercessors showed up. The worship music played as we walked around the conference room, reverencing God's presence. God began to lead us into holding hands. We didn't fully understand what He was doing, but we soon found out that He was making us one in the spirit. It wasn't long before God exposed the devil and every distraction he was using to get the intercessors off focus. The Spirit of God began to explain that we must remain focused as intercessors, letting us know that He can only move through pure and holy vessels. We had to know that we couldn't allow the enemy to weigh us down with the issues of life. It was vital that we remained open to receive our instructions from heaven. Once the Spirit of God ministered to our hearts, we were opened to receive our instructions for the day.

We were instructed to pray for the local ministries in the city. The churches were written down on two sheets of paper, and I was instructed to place the list on the altar. We began to walk around the list of churches as if we were building a hedge of protection. I then fell to my knees, placing my hands on top of each sheet of paper. I began speaking in tongues, lining the lists on top of each other. I moved the two sheets of paper back and forth, binding division and loosing oneness. Then I began to seal the oneness with the blood of Jesus. God was really concerned about the division in the body, and within hours, He had demolished the works of the devil.

It was amazing how God moved through such a small group of intercessors. I can truly say His Word is true. Jesus states in Matthew 18:18-20 (Am)p that, "Truly I tell you whatever you forbid and declare to be improper and unlawful on earth must be what is already forbidden in heaven, and whatever you permit and declare proper and lawful on earth must be what is already permitted in heaven. Again I tell you, if two of you on earth agree (harmonize together, make a symphony together) about whatever [anything and everything] they may ask, it will come to pass and be done for them by My Father in heaven. For wherever two or three are gathered (into) My name, there I Am in the mist of them."

Jesus has truly proven His Word to TAGS Ministries. Our oneness has moved God in radical ways for our city, and I am proud to say that we, as a ministry, have tapped into the fullness of the call. If we had allowed the things that were taking place in the natural to stop us, we wouldn't be sharing these wonderful manifestations of intercession with the world now.

March 24, 2007 marked the fifth prayer service and I can say that God released even more grace. A month had flown by and our level of intercession had grown in leaps and bounds. Once God finds you obeying His instructions, He continues to release power to tear down the strongholds of the enemy. This service brought with it a deeper revelation of who I was in the realm of the spirit. I was instructed to prepare the intercessors for the next phase in the ministry. He revealed the apostolic anointing I walked in and explained the pioneering grace that would be released through The Anointed Gap Standers Ministries. I knew that I was truly hearing from God concerning my life's assignment. I also knew that our intercession was stirring demonic movement like never before.

We walked into the conference room to find nothing set up for our prayer service. There were a few chairs in the room, but they were all different colors. I didn't allow this to stop what God wanted to do through our intercession. I ignored the natural and embraced the supernatural. I knew God was only testing our commitment. My reason for giving my time, energy, and money was for a God move, so we began to tap into worship, exalting God above everything the enemy was attempting to do. God wanted to see if we would stay true to the vision, regardless of the things we had to suffer.

During this season, everything changed for me. Friends who I once could depend on completely stop associating with me. Because I refused to give up on God's vision for my life, things began to change, but my leaning had to be entirely on Him and my trust had to be completely in Him. God made me very dependent on Him because He knew where He was taking me. God made sure that no man could say that it was by his hand that I made it to my Promised Land.

After God finished uncovering the deep things to us regarding TAGS Ministries, we left the conference room.

We went to check on my spiritual mother because she
wasn't able to attend the prayer meeting. While sitting in
her living room searching the scriptures, the Spirit of God
took over my hands and fingers. I felt this supernatural
power that I couldn't began to explain. I could literally feel
the Spirit of God taking the enemy by the neck. I knew
God was pleased with our times of intercession, and He
was letting us know that the battle is always His. We have
to always allow God to give us insight into the deep things
of Him. We must have the ability to see through the eyes
of God, and we must know that it is only the power of God
that will destroy the works of the devil.

April 7, 2007 marked the sixth service held in the
conference room. During this service, the intercessors were
given an opportunity to share what the Spirit of God was
giving them during their own personal prayer time. It was
amazing how God was dealing with everyone concerning
false doctrine. We were instructed to anoint the city's map,
and each intercessor was given the opportunity to intercede
as the Spirit gave them intercessory prayers concerning the
city. He then used my body to release an anointing for the
west of our city. I cried out with everything on the inside
of me for businesses, leaders, churches, families, and
everything and everyone who represented the western
portion of our city. We really allowed God to move
through us during this time of intercession. We were

certain our city was coming into alignment with God's Word.

Saturday, April 14, 2007 marked our seventh and final service in the conference room. This last day consisted of nothing but praise and worship. We thanked Him for being with us through it all. He revealed to us that our intercession had torn down the high places in the city, and He was now anointing us to step boldly into our next phase in ministry.

Walking in Love

May He grant you out of the rich treasury of His glory to be strengthened and reinforce with mighty power in the inner man by the [Holy] Spirit [Himself indwelling your innermost being and personality](Ephesians 3:16 Amp).

I can say with confidence that God is fully capable of giving His people a hunger and thirst for the deep things of Him. He is ready to reveal Himself in ways a natural mind can't begin to understand. He is a God who speaks through everything, and I strongly believe that the natural things were created to give us an image of the spoken Word. It is time we know that it is the spoken Word that will reveal who God is in this earth realm.

After leaving the conference room, we were instructed

to do anointed prayer walks, and our starting area was the western portion of our city. Every Saturday evening, we walked and prayed, and through our obedience, we'd learned what walking in love consisted of. We'd learned that love meant giving ourselves completely to God, and surrendering every part of ourselves to do His will. The manifestation of intercession was amazing. There were times when we stood on church grounds weeping for pastors, binding the enemy off the minds of the leaders in our city. These leaders were men and women of God who we had never met, but yet, we were able to tap into their inner warfare. There were times when we cried out to the Lord to strengthen pastors who were only minutes away from giving up. We identified with their suffering, and our weeping took place like never before. God had TAGS Ministries walking the city in love. We gave ourselves to the Spirit until change took place in the natural. We were able to know the secrets of different families in our city. God allowed us to see demonic activity that only gap standing prayer would reveal. These prayer walks took us into areas that really pulled on our intercession. We wept for our youth. It was weeping that was a sure sign that burdens were being removed and yokes were being destroyed. TAGS was a behind-the-scenes ministry, yet we were out in the community working for the kingdom. Strongholds were being severed from the minds of God's people, and He chose gap standing prayer to get the job done.

I encourage every reader to hear and obey God in every season. Give yourselves to God so He can uncover and reveal His heart directly to you. Regardless of the negative things that were released to stop me, my obedience elevated me into new realms of authority. Once you come into the knowledge of your purpose, it's difficult to sit and wait until something happens. You have to move and make something happen. Purpose has the power to put a run in your spirit, a movement that nothing in this natural realm can stop. Purpose gives you a determination that refuses to be weakened. It brings you into a realm of assured faith. Regardless of what you're facing, purpose projects you into a steadfast hope. Once I came into the knowledge that I was born to intercede, gap standing became my identity. I didn't feel complete unless I was active doing what I was anointed to do. I am not in my place unless I'm in a place of prayer. Once you identify the real you, it is impossible to wear a mask, pretending to be someone else. You will not be complete until you're walking in the fullness of the call.

Purpose puts a drive in you that won't stop until you're sure you're traveling in the right direction. It creates wings of elevation that lifts you above the issues of life. I can go on and on giving illustrations of the power of purpose. Not just the power of purpose, but also the power of knowing your purpose. Everyone is created with purpose in mind, but not everyone is aware of the role they are to play in this earth realm. It takes fearing God to step into the realm of knowing who you are. It takes staying focused on God to complete the assignment He has given into your hands.

I know that everything I've faced in this life was preordained by God. Every failure was something I had to experience to help someone else. Yes, failure was part of the plan. You can walk with your head lifted at all times when you realize your shortcomings have become your victories. You can truly walk with purpose in mind when you know God has been with you through it all. I know I wouldn't be the intercessor I am today had I not experienced difficulties in life. I know that I am who I am only because I never gave up. Regardless of what I had to face, I stayed true to who I was in the realm of the spirit.

My Prayer for You

My prayer for you is that you will position yourself to see truth concerning your destiny, and that you will never allow the opinions of others to limit your God given abilities. I pray that you will boldly enter into the fullness of the call, free of distractions. And that you will boldly present the great investment back to God. I pray you will always know that the One who has begun a good work in you will continue until the coming of Christ. The enemy will always demonstrate his position and it is vital that you release and truly demonstrate yours. God has given you His spirit and I pray that you will release Him with all the boldness and confidence from within. Let nothing, I mean let nothing, rob you of your true identity. I pray you will get in God's presence and remain there until you're sure you are making a difference in the earth realm.

In Jesus name,

Amen.

Chapter 9

Becoming Birthing Channels

Let us all come forward and draw near with true (honest
and sincere) hearts in unqualified assurance and absolute
conviction engendered by faith (by that leaning of the
entire human personality on God in absolute trust and
confidence in His power, wisdom, and goodness), having
our hearts sprinkled and purified from a guilty (evil)
conscience and our bodies cleansed with pure water. So let
us seize and hold fast and retain without wavering the hope
we cherish and confess and our acknowledgment of it, for
He who promised is reliable (sure) and faithful to His Word
(Hebrews 10:22-23 Amp).

It is time for us to take our eyes off our surroundings.
It is the things we see with our natural eyes that hinder us
from progressing in the kingdom of God. We are in this
world, but we are not of this world. The things of this
world shouldn't limit our God given abilities. The enemy
knows and recognizes the power God desires to
demonstrate through us. He also understands the power
and deliverance that comes through our acts of obedience.
The enemy is always plotting, trying everything in his

power to keep us from embracing the fullness of God. He plans to kill dreams and visions before they manifest in the natural. He stirs up things in the natural, causing us to become blind to the truth. He understands that if the people of God embrace truth, they will begin to walk in their exalted positions. Walking in our exalted positions is a very strong force against the enemy because it keeps him in his place of defeat.

The enemy tries everything in his power to keep blinders on the eyes of God's people. He does not want us to come into the knowledge of the truth. The truth tells us that we're more than conquerors in Christ Jesus, regardless of what the outer appearance may be (see Romans 8:37). The truth tells us that old things are passed away, behold, all things are become new (see 2 Corinthians 5:17). As you can see, the truth changes our views on life, giving us the ability to see our expected end.

The devil is a defeated foe who has been stripped of all his power. The only strategy he has is deceit. He gains his control through painted images and by whispering lies to anyone who will hear him. He takes advantage of every opportunity he finds to slither his way into our lives. The Lord has revealed to me that the enemy is establishing seats in ministries. I mean he is sitting back in confidence, knowing the vision shall not come to pass. The only way the enemy can gain this much control is when the body of Christ loses focus. The question is: *How can the people of God lose focus to the point that the enemy is taking over?* This takes place in the body of Christ because we haven't embraced faith with the full assurance. We have to stand regardless of the pictures the enemy has painted for our natural eyes to see. Hebrews 11:1 (Amp) reads, "Now faith is the assurance (the confirmation, the title deed of the things [we] hope for, being the proof of the things [we] do not see and the conviction of their reality [faith perceiving as real fact what is not revealed to the senses."

We can never forget God's avenue of revealing things to His creation. God always reveals things in the spirit, so we can't respond to God promises with a natural response. God's Word is true, and whether you see the evidence of His Word or not, His Word is still true. The Bible also says, in Hebrews 11:3 (Amp), that "by faith we understand that the worlds [during the successive ages] were framed (fashioned, put in order, and equipped for their intended purpose) by the word of God so that what we see was not made out of things which are visible."

We can never step out of the supernatural and into the natural thinking that the vision will come forth. Every vision that is given from God is through spiritual insight. It is going to take the body of Christ embracing the things of the Spirit for the vision to manifest. According to Webster's Dictionary, a vision is *the act or power of anticipating that which will or may come to be; foresight.* If God gives us foresight concerning our lives, He has also empowered us to bring forth what He has allowed us to see. It doesn't matter what we see with our natural eyes, our spiritual visions should give us hope.

The Bible teaches us, in Proverbs 29:18, that where there is no vision, the people perish. A vision should build our confidence in such a way that we know that our lives are getting better. God shows us a better life so we may strive to achieve that life. Once we begin to see the vision, we must put in strenuous efforts to reach our goal. Every vision given by God is given to empower us with a life of determination. To remain determined in the spirit, we must have a certain level of confidence. Being confident is the key! The enemy will always send distractions, and please know that he will send them packed with deceit. It is his job to convince you that the truth about you is a lie, and it is your job to stand on the Word of God with confidence, knowing God will bring every promise to pass.

Since embracing my purpose, I've had many people tell me what I'm not capable of doing, instead of speaking to my capabilities. So, we must be confident regarding what God has spoken concerning our lives. We must stand on

His promises free of distractions. Your visions and dreams are just that: yours! They belong to you! There's not a person on this earth capable of doing what you were created to do. God has strategically set a time and a destination in place just for you. It is my heart's desire that you keep in mind that your adversary will do his part to keep you from reaching that place and time. Know that you must become deaf to the lies sent to hinder you. Keep in mind that God has given you a promise designed just for you. He has also given you a specific route to go, and you must remain on your road to success. Stay focused, keep the promise within view, and march on until you hear those wonderful words: *Well done, my faithful servant.*

Bringing Forth the Vision

Therefore then, since we are surrounded by so great a cloud of witnesses [who have borne testimony to the truth, let us strip off and throw aside every encumbrance (unnecessary weight) and that sin which so readily (deftly and cleverly clings to and entangles us, and let us run with patient endurance and steady and active persistence the appointed course of the race that is set before us (Hebrews 12:1 Amp).

At all times, we should remind ourselves of the cross our Lord endured so we might walk in victory. Jesus died to give us the power to walk as sons and daughters of the

Most High God. We are called to endure hardship and suffering as first class soldiers. Our focus, at all times, should be on pleasing the One who called us out of darkness. There shouldn't be anything of this world powerful enough to cause us to abort the process. Our lives should continue to proclaim what God has promised. We should also take on an attitude against the devil that lets him know that regardless of the struggle, the opposition, or the fight, the vision God has given us shall come to pass.

We can't allow the outer court of our lives to hold us captive. The enemy will always stir up fleshy desires. He is a persistent enemy, and he wants God's people to give up on their promise. He paints pictures of defeat, causing the minds of God's people to accept defeat, instead of victory. The Bible teaches us that faith cometh by hearing, and hearing by the Word of God (Romans 10:17). We lose focus of the sure Word of God because we're not hearing it enough to increase in our faith walk. Once we begin to spend time with God, reminding Him of what He has already promised, our faith begins to increase. During a very immature stage of my Christian walk, God revealed to me that I was born to intercede. I didn't fully understand it then, but God said it, so I embraced it. I invested in literature that would help me understand my position in the realm of spirit. Once I began seeking answers, God began to manifest His will for my life. I remember the first time

He used me to manifest the miraculous. An overwhelming desire to pray for one of my friends had taken over me. I went into warfare for about an hour, and I can remember commanding the devil to take his hands off my friend. I had no idea what was going on with her, and after the intercession, I was too tired to call her and find out. Two days passed before I heard from her. She told me how close she had come to killing her husband. She shared how he was attempting to leave her for another woman, and she'd pulled a knife out to kill him. She also explained how the feeling of rage and anger instantly left her, and she allowed him to leave unharmed. God used this situation to show me how important my purpose was. The day and time I entered into warfare on her behalf was the very same day and time she attempted to take the life of her husband. God was binding the works of the devil, and He chose me to do it through. This experience taught me that God has placed visions and dreams in us for a greater purpose. Lives are depending on our obedience, and it is vital that we see how important our visions and dreams are to the kingdom of God.

When God revealed to me that He was going to use me through book writing, it stirred me to read more. Every time I went into a store, I found myself in the book section. I had a mental picture of becoming a best-selling author. I didn't share my vision with too many people, only the ones

I knew would encourage me. I knew that everyone wasn't aware of the great investment God had placed on the inside of me. It wasn't until I knew that my book was birthed out that I shared it with a larger crowd. During this time, God had built up my confidence in such a way that I didn't need encouragement from anyone. I was certain that writing was a gift God had given me, and no one had the power to take my God given ability. Each day, I would get into God's presence so He would uncover mysteries for my book, and those revelations began to flow through my writing. I can remember questioning God concerning who would publish my material. God informed me that it must be written before it could become published material, so I stopped procrastinating on the gift that was so ready to make room for me. I noticed that each time I lost focus on completing the book, a supernatural force would push me forward. God wouldn't allow me to abort the process. He had predestined me to minister through books, and He wasn't going to allow the plan for my life to die.

After obeying God in something as small as jotting down thoughts, He directed me to the publishing company of His choice. One Saturday while attending a funeral, God began speaking. They opened the floor for expressions from family and friends. The family had chosen a woman by the name of Anna Whitaker. They called her name several times, leaving an echo in my spirit. Even after leaving, I heard this woman's name over and over again. I remained very still because I knew the Lord was calling me to remain sensitive to His next move.

I was then led to visit my spiritual mother. I knew that she was one person I could depend on when it came to moving with God's movement. She was in the process of relocating to Cleveland, Ohio, and she never allows natural things to keep her from embracing the pull of prayer. At this particular time, Mother was filling a box with books, and God began to pull us into the realm of intercession. I was pacing the floor, releasing tongues and my spiritual mother was bent over in a birthing posture. As we reverenced the presence of God in the uniqueness of our gifts, a book in the box captured my attention. It appeared as if God had a magnifying glass on the publishing company. The power of God was very heavy on me. So, I pulled the book from the box with my eyes closed. I didn't want to tap out of this move of God, so I listened very carefully for His instructions. My eyes remained closed as I was led to throw the book in front of my spiritual mother. As she toiled with deep travail, she picked the book up. Tapping into an even deeper level of intercession, she brought the book closer to her heart. God was birthing something out in the spirit that we couldn't begin to grasp in the natural. We were instruments, but yet, totally unaware of what the Great Intercessor was doing.

Once the spirit of intercession lifted, we were free to read the contents of this book. I found out why I couldn't shake the woman's name at the funeral. She had the same name as the publishing company God was leading me to use: *The Whitaker House*. Through this experience, God has taught me the importance of holding fast to the vision. God reveals things in part and we must follow His directions in every season. The Lord wanted me to trust His Word. If He told me I would minister through book writing, it was my job to believe. I was stressing about the publishing company, but God proved to me that He only moves through obedience. Once I obeyed in writing, God gave more instructions. I now know that God calls us out of the world with purpose in mind. He begins to reveal powerful visions and predestined plans to us, visions and plans He hasn't anointed any other soul to see or accomplish. It is our own personal revelation from God. As you walk with Him, He continues to empower you to possess new territories with a full assurance and immediate obedience. The Lord does not show us the whole finished product. He shows us just enough to cause us to run. God takes His time with His chosen vessels, allowing us time to add to our faith the things needed to complete the race. The Bible encourages us to add to our faith virtue, and to virtue knowledge; and to knowledge temperance; and to temperance patience, and to patience godliness; and to godliness brotherly kindness, and to brotherly kindness charity (2 Peter 1:5-7 Amp).

As you can see, faith without works is dead. God graces us with more wisdom as we continue to add to what He has already given us.

God is a progressive God. Gradually, He takes us from level to level, preparing us for our destinies. Every vision given by God starts with a small idea. Once He sees us running with patience toward accomplishing the goal, He begins to overflow us with more ideas and more running power. Once He finds us living a purpose driven life, He begins to give us strategic plans to bring forth the visions.

When you begin to tap into the knowledge that you are full of vision, you must work towards birthing out the promise. We must learn to flow with the Holy Ghost, even if we don't fully understand His movement. We must carry the abundance of the vision, even if it seems too weighty for us. I can remember when God revealed to me that He desired to heal His children through me. I believed it, but I didn't speak it, nor did I attempt to embrace it. I had a tendency of saying things like, "I hear you, Lord, but those are some big shoes to fill." I didn't have a passion when it came to walking in my anointing, but God allowed me to attend Juanita Bynum's Threshing Floor Revival. During this revival, every gift that was lying dormant on the inside of me began to rise up with power. I was sitting beside an anointed woman of God, and even though I didn't know her personally, we were connected in the spirit. Once the Spirit of God began moving in the service, I fell to the floor in reverence of His presence. All I felt in my spirit was a total yes. God used this experience to tap me into everything He wanted to do through me. While I was bowed down in the Lord's presence, He used me to lay hands on the woman of God's right foot. I stayed there weeping and travailing over this woman's foot. I had different people speaking in my ear, but I could only hear God's voice commanding me to surrender all. He told me that lives were depending on me to obey Him. He revealed to me that people were waiting to be healed through the power He desired to release through me. Later that evening, I went back to my hotel room bowed down in spirit. The Lord had really shown Himself mighty in me and through me.

The next day, I ended up sitting on the same level with the woman God used me to lay hands on. There were over 50,000 people at this revival, so I knew meeting her again was 100% divine. God used her to minister to me in a powerful way. She told me that both of her feet were swollen to the point that she couldn't walk without support. Her right foot had completely gone down, but the left one was still swollen. This experience caused me to understand the importance of becoming birthing channels for God. God demonstrated how He desired to bring forth His will through my body. He also showed me how important it was that I release everything He had placed on the inside of me.

God didn't stop building up my confidence in this one experience. Once I returned home, a young lady testified about being diagnosed with cancer. Before leaving for the revival, God had assigned me to pray for her. I used the paper with the diagnosis as a point of contact, but the Sunday following Juanita Bynum's revival, God decided to heal her through my embrace: I hugged her and God instantly healed her body. She returned to the doctor to find out that she was completely cancer free. This really stirred my faith and motivated me to walk daily as a channel of power. To become this channel of power, we must first and foremost forsake our own will. Jesus walked as our perfect example, and He came crying, "Not My Will!" Jesus stated in St. John 5:30 (Amp) that, "I am able to do nothing from Myself [independently, of My own accord ---but only as I am taught by God and as I get His orders]. Even as I hear, I judge [I decide as I am bidden to decide. As the voice comes to Me, so I give a decision], and My judgment is right (just, righteous), because I do not seek or consult My own will [I have no desire to do what is pleasing to Myself, My own aim, My own purpose] but only the will and pleasure of the Father Who sent Me."

St. John 5:30 takes me back to my assignment, an assignment in which faith had to be in operation. God picked out certain intercessors within the city to release prayer, and they had a strong anointing for specific target areas. Everyone God marked for intercession during this time wasn't humble enough to do the will of God, but the ones who obeyed, God manifested Himself as the Great Intercessor through them. My spiritual mother's obedience in this assignment manifested the glory of God in extreme ways. Her target area was addiction, and she really had a heart to cry out for people who were bound by this spirit. I can remember one day she began praying against crack cocaine, and as she moved into intercession, she saw a field of poppy plants. God began to release His power, and she could literally see Him uprooting every plant. She didn't fully understand God's reason for destroying this field of plants at the time, but after doing research on this unique plant, we found out that inside the pod of this plant is the ovary and the ovary produces opium. Opium contains over 50 types of alkaloids, including codeine and morphine. In 1898, diacetylmorphine was substituted for morphine and it was marketed under the brand name heroin. Now, we can understand why God destroyed this field of plants through the power of intercession. Obedience will always deliver amazing results. Jesus is our example, and He had to remain focused on the Father's will to walk in His divine purpose. He remained obedient even to the death of the cross. The power that comes with obedience always eliminates self-will. It helps us embrace the fact that *there is no more I but Christ who lives on the inside.* Our motivation should always be becoming who God created us to be. To be birthing channels for God, we must be willing to change. Change creates new ways for God to bless us. We should be people who are always in position to be used by God. Our availability must be on point at all times. Our time must become God's time, because at all times, we should bring Him glory.

My Prayer for You

My prayer for you today is that you will understand the fullness of who you are, and you will daily walk in the image and the likeness of the Creator, allowing His glory to be revealed through you. I pray you will choose to live a holy and consecrated life, one that will only produce the fruit of the Spirit. I pray your body is truly being reconstructed into a channel of power, and that God will always choose you to birth out His will in the name of Jesus. I pray that faith and obedience has become the moving forces in your life, and through your faith and obedience, your visions and dreams are manifesting right before your eyes. I pray that you are becoming a true channel for the kingdom of God.

In Jesus Name,

Amen.

Chapter 10

Attachments Becoming Strongholds

For the weapons of our warfare are not physical [weapons of flesh and blood], but they are mighty before God for the overthrow and destruction of strongholds, [In as much as we] refute arguments and theories and reasonings and every proud and lofty thing that sets itself up against the [true] knowledge of God; and we lead every thought and purpose away captive into the obedience of Christ (the Messiah, the Anointed One) (2 Corinthians 10:4-5 Amp).

God has given us the authority to speak His Word. It is the same Word that created the world and everything that dwells therein. God spoke, "Let there be," and the Word had to manifest. He has placed dominating power in our mouths, and there is no excuse for the body of Christ to live defeated lives. The time has come that we stand up in God's authority and in the fullness of His power. Standing requires us to know the craftiness of our enemy. We must become aware of his tactics, and we must deal with his tactics in the power of Jesus name.

To display victory, we must also learn our weak areas.

The enemy has studied us, and it is time that we examine ourselves. He is aware of our weaknesses and knows exactly when and how to move in. I know that the devil takes pleasure in my emotions, and it is vital that I maintain balanced in that area. Once I give myself over to my own will, I miss out on functioning properly for the kingdom of God. It is my job to keep my eyes on the promise, regardless of who the devil decides to use against me.

The enemy questions your faith daily, and through his crafty ways, he convinces you to agree with him. All the enemy needs is for you to agree with his lies of defeat. Once he gains control of your thoughts, he can destroy your life. You must maintain a Christ aligned mind. It is the enemy's job to apply pressure to your weakest area. It was the people who I put the most confidence in that the enemy used the most against me, but as long as my thoughts remained on the Word, victory manifested for me. I know God gave the enemy permission to try me when it came to my marriage. It was my marriage experiences that opened my eyes to certain tactics of the enemy. During the first years of my life as a wife, I allowed the lies of the enemy to build up a stronghold in my mind. I could only view my husband through negative eyes. I allowed the lies of the enemy to take a hold of me. The attachments of the devil became strongholds in my life. My thinking was off balance, and the enemy played mind games for years. The season God uncovered this work of the devil, I was given an opportunity to share it with the body of Christ.

This Word was released years ago during an intercessory prayer seminar. God began to reveal how we, as believers, allow the enemy of the mind to rule in our thought processes. God uncovered how the enemy gains and maintains control. One of the intercessors came up to help me with the illustration. We used clothes, pens, and yarn to demonstrate this work of the enemy. Each time a negative word was sown into the mind of the intercessor, his silence caused a pen to be attached to his clothing. As negative words were released, the intercessor stood there, allowing the yarn and pens to form a complete circle. This circle was symbolic of a stronghold in the realm of the spirit. Once this stronghold was formed, I had complete control of his hands and arms. He could not function properly as a soldier. God revealed how silence in the spirit places you in a position of defeat. We are called to be aggressive in the spirit, and we should never allow the devil's lies to attach themselves to us.

Another intercessor came up to demonstrate how victory is always won. Negative words were plucked up from the root each time positive confessions were released. The Word of the Lord completely destroyed every attempt of the enemy. Attachments from the enemy can't consume you if you use your weapon. The Word of God is always our defense, but we must use it during our times of warfare. It is the enemy's job to destroy, and it is our job to detect and slay the works of the devil. It is high time that we know our position through the shed blood of Christ, and it is time we become the representatives that truly demonstrate the power of God in this earth realm.

During the first years of my life as a wife, I remained silent, allowing the enemy to produce fruit in my life. The enemy's lies had a dwelling place in my heart. Instead of speaking and standing on the promises of God, I allowed the enemy to paint images of defeat. It was my job as a representative of Christ to cast down vain images. As Christ representatives, we are to cast down imaginations, and every high thing that exalts itself against the knowledge of God. The images of the devil shouldn't change our views on life. God is a God who can't lie. If He has promised us a strong and successful future, that is the only Word attachment that should surround us. Our experiences are created only to expose the works of the devil, and we must learn to speak the Word, regardless of what appears before our natural eyes. We are fighting a battle that must be defeated in the spirit, therefore, we must have spiritual eyes to see our enemy. The devil is very cunning and sneaky, and to see him, you must be wise. He will slither his way into a conversation in an instant. His goal is to steal, and if you're not in tune with the Word, he will snatch everything God has established you in. He will steal your love, peace, and joy - everything that keeps you producing. The enemy's goal is to sift at your fruit until you have no fruit at all. He does not want to see you productive.

I can recall one morning waking up full of joy. I felt well rested, and was very excited to start my day off in prayer. As I was standing over the sink and washing my face, I saw my mother on her death bed. My mother had recently passed away, and I was trying to overcome the grief I was suffering because of her death. As I was standing there, it seemed as if my life had gone back to that very day. I saw everything that had taken place the day she passed. Tears rolled down my face, and without warning, I saw the enemy. I began to bind the enemy of the mind. I knew he wanted to steal my joy. I began to speak peace, love, joy, and all those blessings God had established in me over myself. I knew I didn't have to yield to the tactics of the enemy. All I had to do was open my mouth. After I finished enforcing who I was in Christ, I knew the enemy felt stupid for even trying that on me. I know that the enemy comes only to steal, kill, and destroy. So, he was on his job; he was just doing what he does, and I was just doing what I do, keeping him under my feet in a place of defeat. I realize that it is my job to praise God in the midst of the storm, and I can't allow the storms of life to discourage me. Why should I allow the enemy to discourage me with something I cannot change? God has granted me the serenity to accept the things I cannot change. He has also given me the courage to change the things I'm able to change, and the wisdom to know the difference. As representatives of Christ, knowing the tactics of the enemy is vital to our survival.

I can recall my sister and I talking. We were enjoying God's Word, and out of nowhere, the devil entered the conversation. My sister began telling me something negative someone had said about me. I sat there in complete silence for a brief moment because I saw the enemy. I began to show her how easily she allowed the enemy to use her. I explained to her that God was doing some things in my life, and I couldn't allow anything negative to enter my spirit. After ministering to her, I began to put the devil in his place. I immediately went to war in the spirit because I had to allow the Greater One to deal with my spiritual enemy. The Spirit of God is always waiting on us to do the things He has called us to do. It is our job to keep the devil under our feet, enforcing who we are in Christ. Yes, I know who I am, and I know I am established in joy, therefore, nothing the enemy tries will cause me to lose my joy.

Once the devil realizes he can't speak directly to your mind to tear you down, he begins using the ones closest to you. The enemy uses our closest companions because he believes this will cause us to lose focus of who we're really fighting. It is very important that we don't allow the things of this world to blind us to the things of the spirit. God is always present and waiting to impart more power to tear down the strongholds of the enemy.

I have captured and recaptured past failures and victories that others may see truth. God is uncovering the truth because it is vital we recognize how the devil creeps into our homes. He does this through false images, dreams, emotions, and anything that will allow him the opportunity to rule our minds. We must guard our minds by instantly detecting demonic invasion. The enemy is a master deceiver. He uses weapons that are crafty enough to twist our thinking. It is his plan to drag us into fighting ghosts: false images that appear to be real. This is why it is vital that we cast down vain imaginations and every high thing that exalts itself against the knowledge of God.

Recognizing Demonic Invasion

So [as the results of the Messiah's intervention] they shall [reverently] fear the name of the Lord from the west, and His glory from the rising of the sun. When the enemy shall come in like a flood the Spirit of the Lord will lift up a standard against him and put him to flight [for He will come like a rushing stream which the breath of the Lord drives](Isaiah 59:19 Amp).

The Lord continues to take us through a process of demolishing the flesh. As believers, we must be empowered to live a lifestyle of walking in the Spirit. Once we begin to yield to our human impulses, key entrances are made for the enemy. When we allow ourselves to waver, we open doors for demonic invasion. God really opened my eyes to this through a dream. In this dream, I was surrounded by complete darkness. I stood over this hole in the ground that was covered by a very heavy steel top. It was a covering that was strong enough to keep everything in. I began to lift this covering, and as soon as the top was off, black snakes ferociously attacked me. After waking from the dream, I heard the Lord speaking, "As long as the door remains closed, the enemy cannot invade your life. He must be given access to your domain." God has given us dominion over the fish of the sea, the birds of the air, and over the cattle, but this is not the most rewarding part, the Word goes on to say, over all the earth and over every creeping thing that creeps on the earth (see Genesis 1:26). Know that God has given you dominion, and if you're living a defeated life, you haven't quite grasped who God has created you to be.

Attachments Becoming Strongholds

I would like to share the story with you about the season the enemy was given access to destroy my life. It was the year I'd decided to enter into marriage out of season. My husband was very nice, and he stood out to me. We worked together, and I admired him because he wasn't seeking the attention of all the women on the job. I admired the fact that I interested him because I was a woman of faith. He couldn't believe that a twenty-two year old woman was serving God. The truth of the matter was I was just getting to know God. I had been saved for two years, and I was still wrestling with a lot of issues in my flesh. I had just recently cut all ties with my oldest daughter's father, and it felt kind of nice to meet someone who was interested in me because of my faith. I found him very attractive, and I started dating him with the hope that he would choose me as his bride one day. I ended up falling in love with him, and four years later, we were exchanging vows. It didn't take us long to realize that neither one of us was ready for marriage. It seemed as if I'd entered the marriage praying for a way of escape. He wasn't living holy, and I had no desire to live any other way, but I didn't want giving up on him to cause others to see me as a selfish individual. My need for a man or anything of the world had changed tremendously because I had accepted my purpose. I was certain I no longer wanted to share my life with someone who didn't love Jesus enough to serve Him. So, I wanted out, and I wanted a very good reason to turn my back on my spouse.

Daily, I opened the door for the enemy to invade my life. Each time I went to God, He instructed me to stay with my husband. I didn't understand God's instructions, nor did I agree with them. Selfishly, I continued to pray for a way out, instead of asking for a heart and a mind to obey the instructions God had already given me. The only thing I wanted to do at that time was to throw in the towel.

I can remember lying before the Lord crying and hoping for a way out. My whole life was consumed with one goal, and that was to leave my husband. This particular night, I had made up in my mind that I wasn't going to stop seeking until God gave me new instructions. After minutes into my sobbing, I heard Yolanda Adams's song ringing from within: *Stay, stay right where you are. Don't move to the left or to the right, but stay right there in the center of my will. And while you're there, pray, pray until you get an answer. Pray until your situation changes. Oh just keep on, just keep on, just keep on praying, until it turn into praise.*
God was letting me know that it was His will that I remained with my husband, and it was my job to pray until I had the ability to accept His will. Regardless of what I felt, the Lord made it plain that my suffering was a part of the plan. God didn't want me to allow surface matters to

abort my destiny. I didn't agree with a lot of things, but God viewed all those things through merciful eyes, and He wanted my prayer life to mature me into seeing it this way as well.

I've learned that prayer really does turn into praise. Prayer has the ability to rescue you from yourself. It brings you into a place of peace when everyone else is experiencing chaos. I couldn't see my husband as someone God wanted me to live my life with. I was aware of the fact that God is all-knowing, and I also knew God wasn't blind to the contrary things my husband continued to do. I was so captured by the things I saw, I lost all hope for a better life, but it wasn't my job to see through natural eyes. It was my job to obey God's instructions and wait until change manifested. God wanted me to see the truth and to learn from every wrong decision I had made prior to accepting Him as Lord and Savior.

The power of prayer had finally reconstructed my life, and my new life manifested a new way of thinking. I conditioned my heart to love my husband regardless of the things that I saw with my natural eyes. God even allowed us to bring another child into the world: Keith Dewan Pearson, Jr. I knew that Keith was the child who would mend all the brokenness in our marriage. Life was getting better for us, and I knew that I could only see better days. I had forgotten about all the times I had prayed for a way out of my marriage, but it was at this very moment that the things I had prayed for manifested in the natural. My way of escape appeared in a season when God had completely delivered me from responding to my emotions. The very thing that I thought I wanted for years caught me by surprise.

A serious storm invaded my life through the door I had opened for the enemy. What do you do in a situation like this? I'll tell you what you do. You accept the fact that this is a door you opened, you must deal with whatever comes flowing in, and you must deal with it in the spirit and not in your flesh. You must maintain your spiritual gaze, focusing on the promises of God, regardless of the pain.

The negative situation that manifested through my husband had enough power to weaken me. A response in the flesh would have caused me to immediately pack my clothes and never look back. Instead, I was willing to work through it all. I believed God would heal me and we could live happily ever after. God is truly a God of His Word. He will not put more on us than we can bear. Test and trials can work wonders if we would only condition ourselves to remain still in the presence of God. Flesh cries with a piercing sound during testing times, and it is our job to recognize the hand of God through it all. Yes, I realize the devil attacked my marriage with power, but I still had to see where I went wrong. I do believe that an enemy had a hand in what could have been the destruction of my marriage, but I also believe I played a part in it also. My husband had to see his faults and shortcomings in this situation as well. I couldn't blame myself because the enemy sent something powerful enough to destroy not only trust, but also our marriage. Keep in mind that the enemy tried Jesus, therefore, we are not exempted from the enemy's attempts (see St. Matthew 4:1-11 Amp).

The situation Jesus went through with Satan lets us know that we are given a choice. Whether the devil shows up with power or not, we are given an opportunity to make the right decision. The door was open for the devil to come in and invade Jesus's life, but He didn't give in to the temptation. Through Jesus's example, we can see that we do not have to give in to the enemy's assaults. Yes, Jesus was tempted with worldly things too, but He still chose the right way. I know I allowed the enemy to invade my life when I continued to listen to his lies concerning my spouse, and within two years of the marriage, I was screaming for a way out, even though I had vowed to remain with my husband until death did us part. Experience has taught me that the key to elevation is seeing yourself. You must see your own mistakes, weaknesses, strengths, and all the things that cause you to fall. It is vital we see the areas in our lives that need God's firm, but loving, hand.

Rooting Out the Negative and Planting the Positive

See, I have this day set thee over the nations and over the kingdoms, to root out and to pull down and to destroy, and to throw down, to build, and to plant (Jeremiah 1:10).

Your words hold power, whether negative or positive. They have the ability to dictate your success in life. If you are trusting God to give you a successful life, you must release words that will create a successful future for yourself. God created us to be distributors in this earth realm, and we must distribute the gifts that are given from our Heavenly Father, and we should never allow our hearts to be contaminated. The words sent from the enemy shouldn't destroy the prophetic Word that was spoken over our lives. We must uproot every word of defeat and plant words of victory, knowing that this process will always come with a fight. You must learn to be determined in the spirit, and you can't give up until you get the right results.

Growing in this life as an intercessor requires determination. Life will always present us with obstacles, but we must always be consumed with God's Word. It will take us living a life of fighting to maintain the confession we made when we accepted Jesus as Lord. Once we step out of the natural mindset and into the things of the Spirit, the fight will then begin. Salvation gives us the power and authority to defend our blood bought rights. If we don't take the time out to apply God's Word, there is no way we can truly embrace all of the things God has for us.

The enemy has some target areas when it comes to the believers who desire to walk in their priestly anointings. He targets our thought lives, putting pressure on our emotions and decision-making. These are areas in our lives we must fight to maintain. There is a Word that ministers directly to any area that the enemy puts pressure on. It is time that we wage war, using the Word of God. The enemy understands he is predestined to hell and he works overtime trying to get us to ignore our places of authority. He presents issues in our lives, trying to get us to take our eyes off God. As intercessors, we must remain firm in the things of God. We must create a life of waging war against a defeated foe.

I feel that it wouldn't be fair to give you instructions to fight without giving you the secrets of waging warfare. We are dealing with some highly organized demons, so it will take us being highly organized to defeat them. Accepting Jesus as Lord came with a great assignment. The Bible says, in Mark 16:15-18 (Amp), to "Go ye into all the world, and preach the gospel to every creature. He that believeth and is baptized shall be saved; but he that believeth not shall be damned. And these signs shall follow them that believe; In my name shall they cast out devils, they shall speak with new tongues; They shall take up serpents, and if they drink any deadly thing, it shall not hurt them; they shall lay hands on the sick, and they shall recover."

So, as you can see, demons must go in the name of Jesus. God has given us the power and authority to wage war through enforcing His name, and enforcing His name cannot be ignored. I mentioned earlier how the enemy puts pressure on our thoughts, emotions, and decision making. Once we open our thought life to the garbage the enemy has to offer, he gains control. If he can get us to put our minds on things that does not edify the body of Christ, he can gain more control in this earth realm. I can recall God speaking to me concerning the power of rooting out and planting. One day, my sister and I were riding from a meeting when the Spirit of God began to minister to us. My sister was complaining about some things she was being faced with. It was amazing how God took over that time of fellowship! He began to expose the devil like never before. I partnered with the Holy Spirit and began interceding on my sister's behalf. I could literally feel deliverance taking place in her soul. The Lord began to speak, "Once you begin to get elevated in the things of the Kingdom to the point that your lifestyle rebukes the devil, he has to come up with a way to sift away the anointing.

He begins to speak negative seeds into your spirit. Now, all Satan needs for the individual to do is water and nourish those negative seeds." Nourishment of the negative seed takes place through meditating about the lie or looking at the situation more than staying focused on God. We must always use our power of rooting out and planting. Once something negative is sown into our spirits, we have to immediately root it out and plant positive seeds. It is vital that we react immediately; we should never accept the lies from our adversary. As long as he's walking about as a roaring lion, seeking whom he may devour, it's imperative that we stay focused.

The Lord has given us dominion, and we must, at all times, maintain this place of authority. Jeremiah 1:10 states, "See, I have this day set thee over the nations and over the kingdom, to root out, and to pull down, and to destroy, and to throw down, to build and to plant." After meditating on this verse of scripture, I was led to define a few words just to help you see yourself as God sees you. The Word "root-out," according to the Webster's Dictionary, means *to pull, tear, or dig up by the roots*. It means to *remove completely (utterly, entirely)*. The words "pull down" means to *draw downward, demolish, wreck, and to lower or reduce*. The word "destroy" means to *put an end to, extinguish, to slay, or kill it*. It means to *render ineffective or useless; neutralize, invalidate*. It also means to *defeat completely*. The word "build" means to *develop or increase, to improve the strength or health of.* The last word is "plant", and it means to *place or station with great force or determination* (Reference: Webster's Dictionary).

We have the power to pull up every negative seed planted in our minds by the enemy. We have the power to remove those words completely. We can put an end to it, kill it, slay it, and render those negative seeds ineffective and useless. God has given us the power to completely defeat the enemy, the very enemy who comes only to steal, kill, and destroy. We have been empowered to demolish every work of the wicked one. Once we have done all of the rooting out, pulling down, and destroying, we can then improve the strength of the total man by planting the Word of God. The Word will place us in a position of stability, keeping our minds and hearts on the One who has given us the power of rooting out the negative and planting the positive.

My Prayer for You

My prayer for you today is that you recognize the power and authority that has been given unto you. I pray that not only do you recognize your authority, but I pray that you also put it to work in your life. It is God's desire that you maintain a life of being strong in the Lord and in the power of His might. It is His desire that you forever walk in your exalted position, keeping the devil in his place of defeat. I pray that you refuse to allow any of the enemy's plots to prevail in your life, and that you continue to be steadfast in the things of God, recognizing all the tactics of the enemy. I pray, in Jesus name, that you always defeat your adversary by immediately plucking up the negative that is sown into your life. I pray that attachments from the enemy are a thing of the past, and that strongholds of the mind will never make a home in your heart.

This I pray in Jesus name.

Amen.

Chapter 11 ·

Ministering Through Experience

And do not [for a moment] be frightened or intimidated in anything by your opponents and adversaries, for such [constancy and fearlessness] will be a clear sign (proof and seal) to them of [their impending] destruction, but [a sure token and evidence] of your deliverance and salvation, and that from God. For you have been granted [the privilege] for Christ's sake not only to believe in (adhere to, rely on, and trust in) Him, but also to suffer in His behalf (Philippians 1:28-29 Amp).

It wasn't until God commanded me to write the story of my life that I truly began to understand God's process. I was certain that I had shared everything God wanted me to share in this manuscript. I opened up the first chapter by pouring out my life's experiences after salvation, but God revealed to me that I must share the life I endured before He saved me. Everything I had gone through before receiving Christ as Lord and Savior had a major impact on my decision-making.

God used the years I lived with my father to uncover

the truth about my growth process, and my understanding was truly enlightened. For the majority of my childhood, I witnessed my father abusing my stepmother. She'd become pregnant and aborted several children during these terrible cycles of abuse. I later learned that my mother had gone through the same treatment while she carried me. I was told that I was born with bruises and couldn't stop crying. Through this recap, I learned that life begins before you exit the womb. My God process started during the months my mother carried me. My life was surrounded by people who didn't know their worth, so I grew up not knowing mine. I had watched my mother seek love in men and my stepmother accepted love in the form of abuse. I walked well in both of their shoes. I embraced the first man who'd told me he loved me. Unfortunately, this man was an expressed image of my father. I dated him for years, and my life was filled with sleepless nights and chaotic days. I didn't have the opportunity to know love because all I had ever experienced was hatred. I started dating at the age of sixteen, and I'd become pregnant and miscarried my first child during this time. So, why am I telling my story? I know that some hurting and confused young lady is seeking approval in a man, and some lost teenager is being abused by a confused young man. My advice to you is to get out now! You are too precious in the eyes of God to allow anyone to damage your temple. I'd dated my abuser throughout high school, and by the time I became a senior in high school, I was carrying his child, which, of course, was my second pregnancy. I thank God that the pregnancy didn't abort my destiny. The whole time I carried my child, the Lord kept her father away from me and I was graced with the presence of a real man. I didn't know how to accept him because this was unfamiliar to me. He didn't have hidden motives for being my friend; he just loved my company. God used him to demonstrate to me a better life. Each night, I went to bed smiling instead of crying. Even though someone better was presented to me, I was too bound to embrace him. I didn't have enough wisdom to know that God was delivering me from the hands of the enemy. I didn't have enough hope to embrace a new life. I was robbed of the fight God had put in me; at least, that is what I thought. God sent someone into my life to help heal the hurt, and I was too bound to accept him. The day I delivered my child was the day I ended my relationship with my friend. I ignored the fact that he introduced to me something better. I ran from the unfamiliar to find myself right back in the hands of the enemy: the familiar.

As we go through God's process, we are commanded to let go of the familiar. God opens our eyes to a whole new dimension and truth surfaces with power. The Lord often showed me how I continued to allow my carnal way of thinking to lead me. He revealed how I governed my life according to the dictates of my flesh. I cannot share this information without involving my marriage. After being saved for only a couple of years, I felt that I had to marry to live holy. Instead of embracing Jesus as the answer, I embraced marriage. I was still wounded from past hurts, and was too confused to know exactly what I wanted. I didn't give myself a chance to mature in the things of God. I was damaged and seeking a man to heal the hurt.

I entered into marriage selfishly. I walked into something major during a very immature stage of my life. I was still searching for my identity, and had no idea that one day I would be a world changer. I chose a mate during my then present state of mind, never thinking about my future, but destiny has a way of drawing you into God's perfect will, even when your emotions don't agree. Once I began to embrace purpose, my husband began screaming for the woman he'd married, but she was long gone. We went through a season where he screamed for the old and I held on tightly to the new. There was serious warfare going on between my husband and I. I was certain that the confused and hurting young woman had been put to death, never to rise again. The prophet for the nations was on the scene, ready to tap into her next level. I began to hear the voice of righteousness saying, "Stay focused because destiny is right ahead."

During this time, my marriage was really on shaky

ground. My husband and I had attempted to throw in the towel on many occasions, but hope gave me a determination that refused to be weakened by trials, test, or hardships. I knew that I was anointed to love strong, even in the midst of a hell-storm. I was about to go forth in ministry, and the enemy was hitting my marriage on every side.

Once I entered the now season of my life, it was vital that I had spiritual sight. I realized I had to function according to God's will, regardless of what I wanted. I can remember asking God if losing my marriage was a part of the process. He responded by saying that I would lose everything that didn't line up with His perfect will. This season was ordained by God, and a crucifixion of my heart took place like never before. He began to cut away things in my life that couldn't enter into my next season. This is the process when flesh really begins to die. This is a time that God shows you if your yes really means yes.

I entered this time of my life seeing the filthiness of my flesh and the weakness of my spirit. I had enough spiritual sight to see everything that had to be eliminated in my life. God was commanding me to see and respond according to His will. It didn't matter how emotionally disturbed I had become, God was commanding me to yield totally to Him. It didn't matter about the things I was experiencing in the natural, I had to function solely in the spirit. God was using my life's experiences to build a strong woman of God, and He had to bring balance to my emotions. There is no way you can fight effectively when you're responding to spiritual problems using natural remedies. I was sure that I was making progress in the spirit, even though I wanted to give up on a marriage God commanded me to remain in. I had a consistent life of praying for my marriage, but I was only releasing my own desires during prayer and not the will of God, so my prayers never yielded positive results. I cried out for oneness one day, and screamed for a way of escape the next day. I was very double-minded in my thinking, only because I failed to accept God's will for my life. I allowed destruction to enter into a home that could have been filled with love and peace. Truth was the only thing I had in that season. I had to be truthful with myself. God was speaking, and He was commanding my ears to hear and my heart to receive. Regardless of the pain, truth has a way of getting us through the hardest battles. In that new season, God was waking up the unknown in me, and the untapped power of God was being placed on display. God needed me to be steadfast and unmovable when it came to my husband. There was a serious stretching going on in my members, and regardless of the discomfort, the plans of God were being presented through it all. For years, I had responded to my marriage issues through the eyes of the flesh. I spent many years being unstable even though God continued trying to give me something that was vital to my ministry and life: stability. I must say that there comes a time in our lives that we are commanded to see truth. Through a ten year process of tests and trials, I can now cry with words of wisdom and trust God through it all. It didn't matter how I tried to ignore God's plan, it seemed to have a piercing cry in my life. I held on for years, hoping that light would penetrate the darkness in my life.

I hoped and believed strongly for a better marriage, but it never seemed to manifest. I believed that prayer would manifest change, regardless of the lifestyle my husband wanted to live. I truly thought that I was growing closer and closer to the light, but the more I operated out of my emotions, the darkness continued to get a little darker day by day. It was impossible for me to see a better life operating in my flesh. I know that God allowed me to marry because He knew the suffering wouldn't kill me, and He knew my ability to learn, grow, and release through my life's experiences. There is no other cry like a cry of experience. There is no other journey like one walked out. Through my tests and trials, new levels of wisdom, knowledge, and understanding were birthed out. I now have an extreme level of confidence in my ability to help others. Through everything I've suffered, elevation in the spirit has wrapped itself around me as a protective garment.

I have learned that God will allow us to walk into the fire so He can control the thermostat through it all. He has a way of allowing the heat of the flames to purify us. Instead of coming out with burns, we come out as white as snow. God allows the flames to scorch everything that is contrary to His will, and then, He places a seal of approval upon us, a mark that lets the world know that we are qualified to be His ambassadors.

I must say that the pain of this process came with enough force to weaken my own abilities. The darts from the enemy changed my heart from a stony one to one of flesh. I am certain that during this journey of tests and trials, I have been given a heart for the will of the Father. We go through when we are drawn away by our own desires, but God has a way of forgiving us. He has a way of dusting us off and commanding us to do things His way for the rest of our lives. I went into my marriage with a hope that my lifestyle would change the desires of my husband. I've learned that you can only change yourself. Regardless of the power that is released through you, you must keep in mind that you can only change yourself. For years, I pointed out contrary things in my spouse, hoping that he would change. I failed to realize that it was my job to eliminate contrary things in my own life. We must fight to live a life that pleases God. Daily, we must die to our flesh for God to show us our shortcomings. Newness comes only when we learn to fight against the torments of our pasts. A better life comes only when we step into the unfamiliar, allowing the power of the new environment to erase the hurt. Salvation comes to give us the ability to see past the hurt and embrace hope. I shared my life to help God's creation know that we can't change our pasts, but we can embrace Jesus with all our hearts, and He will freely give us a better life.

Change is Good, So Go Forward!

When Pharaoh drew near, the Israelites looked up, and behold, the Egyptians were marching after; and the Israelites were exceedingly frightened and cried out to the Lord. And they said to Moses is it because there are no graves in Egypt that you have taken us away to die in the wilderness? Why have you treated us this way and brought us out of Egypt? Did we not tell you in Egypt, let us alone; let us serve the Egyptians? For it would have been better for us to serve the Egyptians than to die in the wilderness Moses told the people, Fear not; stand still (firm, confident, undismayed) and see the salvation of the Lord which He will work for you today. For the Egyptians you have seen today you shall never see again. The Lord will fight for you, and you shall hold your peace and remain at rest. The Lord said to Moses, Why do you cry to Me? Tell the people of Israel to go forward (Exodus 14:10-15 Amp).

There are times when God has to take us out of the familiar to bless us. Oftentimes, we don't realize the importance of change. A change of environment can tap us into new and improved ideas. Going after a more rewarding job or trusting God for the perfect mate should be our pursuit. We should never accept the damaging results of our pasts when God has shown us a place of deliverance. Once we learn to deny ourselves, the blessings of God are added to our lives in an amazing way. We pray, "Lord, enlarge our territory", and the Lord responds by saying, "Go and possess new land." The problem is we haven't tapped into the power God has given us and God has given us the ability to possess. So, our actions should always be actions that represent the King. We shouldn't settle for what Egypt has to offer when there is newness in a land flowing with milk and honey. We can peep into our futures; we can look into our places of blessings, never doing what it takes to enjoy the promise. If our destinations are promised lands, that means God has already given us complete ownership of those lands. Some of us are just standing back, looking at the promise, never building up enough courage to embrace what is rightfully ours.

We have to see ourselves as Christ sees us. He is pushing us to possess new lands. He is pushing us to allow our gifts to make room for us. Some of us are anointed to change the world. We're sitting on gifts that are screaming to come out. Our next level is waiting on us to step out and just do it. We are King's kids, and every day of our lives, we should be living like we're serving the King of kings and the Lord of lords. There are times when we allow fear to keep us from the blessings that God is pushing us to possess. Fear can cause us to get comfortable where we are, when we know that so much more lies ahead. We settle for our present state because it takes us doing something different to obtain the promise. Once God begins to do new things in our lives, we take it upon ourselves to believe that we were better off in the old. God cannot do with you in the old what He desires to do with you in the new. We serve a God that is always encouraging us to go forward because He desires to show us new things.

In Exodus 14:15, God had to instruct Moses to speak victory into the hearts of the Israelites. Through the eyes of the natural, a spirit of defeat had invaded their minds. They began to complain during the journey to the Promised Land. As they traveled, they were faced with a few distracting bumps in the road, distractions that were there only to draw their minds back to the God who had shown up in power on many occasions. God was waiting on His children to put victory on their lips. They had to learn to embrace the spiritual, but to do this, they had to lose their grip of the world. Responding to what they saw was the only way they knew to respond. So, to embrace the spiritual, change had to take place. The familiar had to be done away with for them to move into the things of God.

I believe the wilderness experience is the process we must go through to increase in this faith walk. God expects us to stay focused in the midst of the storms. It is our job to keep our eyes on the God who gave us a cloud by day and our fire by night. We must remain faithful to our God, a God who fed us manna from heaven. We must keep in mind that we have to successfully walk through our dry seasons to see the hand of God. To reach our final destinations, we must walk into the unfamiliar. We must remain fixed on the things of God when change seems hard to embrace. God has given us everything we need to make the necessary changes so that we can enjoy all that He has promised. At all times, we must make ourselves available to be used by God, giving our attention only to the things that will help us bring forth purpose. We must remain holy and pure enough to hear every direction from our Heavenly Father, and we must learn to trust Him with every fiber of our being. Our ability to step into the unfamiliar rewards us with the blessings we were created to possess. God uncovers His truths on various levels and restores our hope like we've never experienced. He is always waiting on us to trust Him enough to move into the realm of the unknown. It takes faith and courage to move on this level, but know that change is always good because it keeps us moving forward. Additionally, it delivers us from making circles in the wilderness. I encourage you to boldly walk into your place of blessings with complete trust in God.

My Prayer for You

My prayer for you today is that your faith will move you into the unfamiliar and that your feet will move swiftly towards the place called destiny. I pray that the spirit of fear is a thing of the past and your mind is truly embracing change. No longer will you be afraid to move into new realms of faith and authority. I pray your awareness of who you are is pushing you into new arenas, and you are meeting every person who is assigned to your life, as well as reaping the benefits that come with living a righteous life. No longer are you shackled by the past. You are now realizing that change is good, and you are boldly moving forward.

In Jesus Name,

Amen.

Chapter 12

Tapping into the Mystery of Who You Are

But you are a chosen race, a royal priesthood, a dedicated nation. [God's] own purchased, special people, that you may set forth the wonderful deeds and display the virtues and perfections of Him Who called you out of darkness into His marvelous light (1 Peter 2:9 Amp).

The true reward of salvation is having the ability to see who God created you to be. When you visualize and embrace the truth about yourself, nothing is impossible. Regardless of the words that are released to destroy your life, you are on a firm foundation that is not easily shaken when you know who you are in Christ Jesus. Seeing on this level keeps your eyes fixed on the Lord and your ears sensitive to His voice. Once you walk into this kind of revelation, the only direction you seek is from the throne of God. You know that God is the One who created you and He sent His Son to die for you. He filled you and placed a great assignment within you. This level of seeing places you in the very presence of God. It catapults you into a realm of the unseen, and surface matters don't stand a chance. Regardless of the attacks, your language pushes back the forces of darkness. You are now speaking the uncompromising Word of God. You are releasing the name of Jesus so powerfully that it causes demons to tremble. Your walk is different because you know you are truly housing the Anointed One, and you also know that the anointing is released through your person to destroy yokes and remove burdens. A reward is granted in this realm of knowing. Burdens can't rest upon a person who abides in the presence of God; they are immediately removed. This means you can live a life of peace on earth. You are introduced to a life of no more worries, and you can boldly enjoy the benefits of heaven right here on earth. Yes, peace, joy, and the love of God can manifest before you transition to heaven.

A mystery is something that can only be uncovered by God, so the fact that you are a mystery demolishes the opinions of others. It changes the world's view of you; it even changes your own personal view of yourself. Every word that comes to destroy you is demolished instantly when the mystery of who you are is revealed. God created you, and in His presence, He releases the truth about you. This even destroys the limitations that spiritual leaders have placed on you. So, coming to Jesus; I mean really giving Him your heart, unlocks mysteries. Do you desire to know why God created you? The answer is found through having a personal relationship with Him. Man does not have the ability to uncover and reveal, only God can. It is my desire that this chapter wakes up a desire in you, a stronger desire to know the whole truth and nothing but the truth.

God often used the life of His Prophet, Jeremiah, to speak to me. Because this book blesses me so much, I know that it will speak volumes to the lives of God's people. In Jeremiah 1:5 (Amp), God speaks expressively to Jeremiah, letting him know his position in the realm of the spirit. He said, "Before I formed you in the womb I knew [and] approved of you [as my chosen instrument], and before you were born I separated and set you apart, consecrating you, [and] I appointed you a prophet to the nations."
Once I read and began to meditate about that Word, I was able to see myself through the eyes of God. Immediately, I started ministering to myself. I began to tell myself that the Lord knew me before I entered into the dispensation of time. He created me in His image and likeness and impacted me with divine purpose. I was chosen to do a great work for the kingdom of God before the world knew me. I had a name and an assignment before I was ever a twinkle in my mother's eye. Time awaited the moment to see divine purpose when I came forth out of the womb.

Once you learn to yield to the divine will of God, you

are given a supernatural ability to see through the eyes of God. When God looks at us, He sees purpose, divine power, and all the things He has strategically assigned to our lives. The Lord does not see us through the painted images the world creates for us. The world limits the move of the Spirit. The world's system disregards the divine assignment God has placed upon our lives.

It is the devil's job to keep the eyes of the people of God blinded to the truth. He knows that if we accidentally find out that we were born to win, we'll keep him and all his demon hosts in their places of defeat. The devil only wins when we fail to embrace our kingdom benefits. He wins when we fail to grow closer to the Creator of all things. He wins when we fail to embrace the power God has invested in us. It is what we don't know that keeps us in bondage, and it is what we know and refuse to apply that keeps us in a place of defeat.

The Word was given to instruct and show us the way. The divine Word of God has been given to us, and it is our spiritual inheritance. You are everything the Word of God says you are, and you can do everything the Word of God says you can do. Why do you get God's benefits? Because you were wise enough to read and follow all of the instructions! The Word guarantees us access to the abundant life if we choose to do everything that is written.

In Jeremiah 1:7 (Amp), the Lord commanded Jeremiah to change his language. It states, "But the Lord said to me, say not I am only, a youth; for you shall go to all, to whom I shall send you, and whatever I command you, you shall speak."

The Lord encouraged Jeremiah to stop giving power to the lies and the limitations of the world, and He commanded him to give birth to the deep and hidden things in his heart. Jeremiah had to first speak the Word to see his worth. His words had to come into alignment with God's Word. He was permitted to say only what God commanded him to say. God's Word is the only thing powerful enough to demolish the world's view. It will take us saying what God says about us to see the truth. The spoken Word gives divine revelation to the eternal plans of God. The only assurance we need is that the Word of God is our source of power. If God has given us His Word, He has also given us the ability to make a difference. The Word of God is God Himself, so once we tap into the principle of speaking the Word, we have tapped into the act of releasing God into the earth realm.

Once we begin to truly demonstrate the power and authority of the Word, we must remain focused. We cannot allow our surroundings to cause us to sit on God's anointing. The people we interact with on a daily basis won't understand God's ordained plan for our lives. In

Jeremiah 1:8, the Lord encourages Jeremiah not to be afraid of the faces of the people. It states, "Be not afraid of them [their faces], for I am with you, whatever I command you, you shall speak."

He couldn't allow the negative things that surrounded him to change his view of himself. It was his job to believe the Word and walk in it with steadfast hope. It was also important for him to seek the promises of God, and not what the world had to offer.

I often think about my God ordained assignment. I know if I take my eyes off the author and the finisher of my faith, I'll miss out on accomplishing the task that is set before me. I also realize that I must continue speaking what God says and not what man is saying. I know the vision is too great for a natural mind to comprehend and I must remain in the spirit. I am aware of the fact that the manifestation of the assignment is hidden behind God's cloud of glory. It is vital that we stay in the very face of God and not in the faces of unbelief and doubt. I know God has anointed me to see beyond all that is natural. He has opened my spiritual eyes to see the deepness of His move in the earth realm. There is no way a carnal mind can complete the task that needs to be accomplished. God has given us power to bind and loose, but we must have the eyes to see what needs to be dealt with in the realm of the spirit. Jeremiah 1:10-11 (Amp) states, "See, I have this day

appointed you to the oversight of the nations and of the kingdom to root out and pull down, to destroy and overthrow to build, and to plant. Moreover, the word of the Lord came to me saying, Jeremiah, what do you see? And I said, I see a branch or shoot of an almond tree [the emblem of alertness and activity blossoming in late winter]."
We must have the ability to see to act. To make an impact in this world, our spiritual sight must be intact.

Our fights originate from demonic forces working in the unseen realm. The Bible states in Ephesians 6:12 that we wrestle not against flesh and blood, but against principalities, against powers, against the rulers of the darkness of this world, against spiritual wickedness in high places. The key to overcoming is having the ability to hold fast to the things of the spirit. There is no way Jeremiah would have walked in his exalted position without having spiritual sight. God had given Jeremiah eyes to see every problem when it came to the nations and the kingdoms. He was already anointed for the job; he just had to tap into the mystery of who he was.

In Jeremiah 1:12 (Amp), the Lord lets Jeremiah know that his vision is clear. It states, "Then said the Lord to me, you have seen well, for I am alert and active, watching over My Word to perform it." The Lord was letting Jeremiah know how important it was that he stayed focused on the spoken Word. God will perform as we stand and release His Word in the earth realm. Once Jeremiah began to tap into the spirit realm, his eyes began to gaze toward his destiny. Jeremiah 1:13 (Amp) states, "And the Word of the Lord came to me the second time, saying, what do you see? And I said, I see a boiling pot and the face of it is [tipped away] from the north [its mouth about to pour forth on the south on Judea.]"

Once Jeremiah allowed the Word to direct his sight, he began to grasp eternal destiny. Once the Word of God becomes active and alert in our lives, we can then embrace our preordained assignments. Jeremiah's assignment became clear once he positioned himself to walk through God's process.

Jeremiah 1:14-16 (Amp) states, "Then the Lord said to me, Out of the north the evil [which the prophets had foretold as the result of national sin] shall disclose itself and break forth upon all the inhabitants of the land. For, behold, I will call all the tribes of the kingdoms of the north says the Lord, and they will come and set everyone his throne at the entrance of the gates of Jerusalem, against all its walls round about, and against all the cities of Judah [as God's judicial act, a consequence of Judah's wickedness. And I will utter My judgments against them for all the wickedness of those who have forsaken Me, burned incense to other gods, and worshiped the works of their own hands [idols]."

God began to show Jeremiah how present He was in the affairs of the world, giving him the ability to tap into His heart. Once Jeremiah's gaze began to be on the will of God, He was able to embrace the deep things of God. He had to first know the heart of God before he could effectively work for the kingdom. Jeremiah had to know the hurt as well as the wrath God had for the acts of sin. There is no way we can be His spokesperson without first taking on His heart. Once you know exactly how God desires you to deal with certain acts of sin, you can boldly proclaim His Word.

Once Jeremiah positioned himself to get all of God's instructions, he was ready to go forth in ministry. Jeremiah 1:17 (Amp) states, "But you, [Jeremiah], gird up your loins! Arise and tell them all that I command you. Do not be dismayed and break down at the sight of their faces, lest I confound you before them and permit you to be overcome."

As you can see, it is vital that we walk with God, allowing Him to prepare us for the assignment. Jeremiah had to be equipped for the assignment; he had to also understand his position in the realm of the spirit and what he would come up against. Once Jeremiah's eyes were opened to his exalted position, he was a magnet for demonic attack. Jeremiah 1:18 (Amp) states, "For I, behold I have made you this day a fortified city and an iron pillar and bronze wall against the whole land-against the [successive] kings of Judah, against its princes, against its priest, and against the people of the land [giving you divine strength which no hostile power can overcome]."

Jeremiah wasn't able to walk in his divine assignment until he positioned himself to hear from heaven. We must posture ourselves in the spirit to receive divine counsel. It is time that we eliminate the limitations of the world and accept how God views us. We are spiritual beings made in the image and likeness of God, created by the very hands of God to accomplish a preordained assignment. God makes it clear that it was His hands that made us. As long as we walk in God's perfect will, no hostile power will overcome us. Once you truly embrace the spiritual, nothing can break your focus. Your gaze remains regardless of the attacks. Your level of knowing who you are rebukes the devil, placing you in a stable posture, a place of victory.

Our place of victory does not eliminate the fight. God never told us that we wouldn't have to fight, He just always promised victory. Jeremiah 1:19 (Amp) states, "And they shall fight against you, but they shall not [finally] prevail against you, for I am with you, says the Lord to deliver you."
Now is the time that we step into our divine assignments in

full assurance, knowing that God is with us. I believe the process Jeremiah walked through is the journey for the believer. We must learn to do things according to God's will to receive our abundant lives. There was a place I had to be for God to reveal The Anointed Gap Standers Ministries to me. God knew that TAGS Ministries was in my belly because He placed it there, so He had plans for my life. He knew everything I would have to face to become the vessel He was calling me to be.

I've learned that embracing your spiritual assignment introduces you to a strong life of hearing the voice of God. It places a demand on you to walk by faith and not by sight. The thing He's commanding you to do will introduce you to the unfamiliar. A part of you knows that God wouldn't command you to do something you're not equipped to do, yet fear seems to grip you. Your natural side is at odds with your spiritual side because God is giving you instructions to transition into a place you've never been. You can literally feel warfare stirring in your inner man.

Transitioning from the familiar to the unfamiliar is an act of faith. It's supernatural. A natural mind can't begin to grasp the events that occur in the realm of the spirit, and when a natural mind tries to comprehend spiritual things, our walks may feel like moments of stillness, places of stagnation, and barriers that don't allow a constant flow.

Transitioning by faith is the swift movements of God, the places of manifestations and victories that leaves us speechless. Although uncertainty is the only thing that surrounds us, yielding to the will God demands our levels of faith to perform for us. It places us on a stable, yet invisible ground and our spiritual eyes are commanded to perform for us. Our total surroundings are stressful and chaotic, but our spiritual eyes keep us in places of peace.

Let Nothing Stop You!

Therefore, my beloved brethren, be firm (steadfast), immovable, always abounding in the work of the Lord [always being superior, excelling, doing more than enough in the service of the Lord], knowing and being continually aware that your labor in the Lord is not futile [it is never wasted or to no purpose](1 Corinthians 15:58 Amp).

You must learn to go after God until you're totally aware of who you are in the realm of the spirit. You must see your greatness and walk in it with strong confidence. Rely on God because He is the only one capable of helping you to view yourself with spiritual eyes. Once the Creator has defined you, let nothing or no one stop you. You serve a God who commands you to release the great investment He's placed in you. The things God has assigned to your life is like no other assignment that you'll ever receive. Your assignment is tailor made just for you, and it is very important to the kingdom of God. You must know that God is totally against you allowing natural things to stop you. There is a supernatural abundance on the inside waiting on you to discover that it's there.

I want to issue a warning here: your ability to see your greatness will stir up demonic movement like never before, but once you know who you are, your ability to walk in it will be supernaturally increased. Your assured faith gives you a confidence in the realm of the spirit, and as long as you remain in the spirit, your lifestyle alone will ward off the naysayers. Your focused mind will release warfare against the enemy. Keep in mind that it is his job to side track your thinking. He has a goal, and his goal is to cause you to miss your season.

Reader, I encourage you to remain fixed on the words God spoke concerning you. Know that it is your job to keep the prophecy alive. Know your worth and keep your eyes straight before you. Continue to walk the path that assures you a good future, and never allow the naysayers to get you off track; never allow them to change your language. A lot will be said to stop your progress, so be sure to seek God until you are able to grasp what it is that He's saying about you. Let God's Word be the ultimate and final authority in your life. Walk with a confidence that can't be shaken and move into the realms and arenas God has ordained for your life.

Stay focused and prepare for warfare. Don't waste time defending yourself, let your lifestyle alone defend you. Yes, on the surface, noses will turn up and jealousy will be released, but nothing in the natural can stop a person who remains in the spirit. Your focus on your assignment will cease all the surface matters that tries to take flight in your life. You are secured as long as Jesus is your focus. We are encouraged to overlook the faces of the people. In Jeremiah 1:8, we were forewarned about people who will not receive the great investment. Yes, there will be negativity in the house of God, but keep in mind that you must allow the anointing to change a negative atmosphere. Never allow a negative atmosphere to change you. It is the anointing you release that destroys yokes and removes burdens. So, it is my desire that you maintain your spiritual focus and become the instrument in this earth realm that God has created you to be.

My Prayer for You

My prayer for you today is that you will really embrace the spiritual, allowing God to uncover and reveal the truth about you. I pray that every lie that has limited you in this earth realm is being demolished in Jesus name. I pray your eyes are seeing that the sky is the limit to what you can have, and I pray that you are being stirred to embrace the fullness of who you are. I pray that the untapped power within you is being released right now in Jesus name, and that God is placing movement in your feet and power in your speech. I pray that He's giving you a steadfast momentum that can't be stopped.

In Jesus Name,

Amen.

Chapter 13

The Past, Present, and Future

To everything there is a season, and a time for every matter or purpose under heaven (Ecclesiastes 3:1 Amp).

We must learn to be sensitive to our seasons with an attitude of letting go. As God moves us into new seasons, everything and everyone can't transition with us. Your next season will bring a fresh look. It will also place a command on you to embrace the things that will produce fruit in your life. You must let go of the old, knowing that God is introducing something better and more exciting. The things that once slowed you down are not welcomed in this new place. Situations that once broke your focus are being demolished and God is giving you a steady gaze.

The negative things that once clouded our minds must be done away with. There is no time for decrease when God is commanding increase. There is no way we can see a better life if we're constantly looking back at the things that damaged us. We can't allow old things to stagnate us and kill our progress. Yes, we've made mistakes in the past, and the only way those mistakes can have power is through memories. There is something better before us, and the only way we can enjoy it is by embracing our new places in God. The place that we can see and feel within ourselves is our places of promise. Our promised lands are waiting on us to arrive, and the length of the journey to get to our promised lands has been placed in our hands. So, whether we forgive ourselves today or this time next year, the point of our arrival depends on us.

God has placed a command on us to let go of past hurts, pains, and disappointments, and He is saying press forward into the place that rewards you with the prize. We spend years fighting things we can't change. We find ourselves in a tug-of-war between our pasts and our futures. As we grasp our past failures, sins, and disappointments, we find it hard to gain enough strength to press toward the mark. It is time that we take on the same mindset Paul illustrated in Philippians 3:13-14 (Amp). He states, "I do not consider brethren, that I have captured and made it my own [yet]; but one thing I do [it is my own aspiration]: forgetting what lies behind and straining forward to what lies ahead, I press on toward the goal to win the [supreme and heavenly] prize to which God in Christ Jesus is calling us upward."

God really dealt with me about the power we give our pasts, and He gave me a series of revelations. I can remember waking several times to change positions. I was six months pregnant with my son, and I was going through some serious lower back pains. I knew that sleeping on my back was causing this problem. The weight of the placenta was putting too much pressure on my back, and this was interrupting my ability to maintain my balance. One morning, I woke up pouring my heart out to God. I asked Him, *Lord, why can't I stay off my back?* I knew that the weight of the baby was literally crippling me. There were times when the pain in my back was so intense that it almost knocked me to my knees. Even though sleeping on my back was the most comfortable position, I paid for it dearly.

The Lord began speaking, "This is the condition of my body. My people love the backwards approach, even though they know it brings them pain, just like the weight of the baby makes it difficult for you to walk and maintain balance. Turning to those things that are behind does the same to your spiritual walk. It cripples you, causing the enemy's fiery darts to penetrate you. It leads you into a life of being unstable in your Christian walk." The Lord really wanted me to understand the power that we give the things that lies behind, and He couldn't have used a more powerful illustration. The Lord continued to give me revelation through my pregnancy. He explained that when you're pregnant with purpose, you can't take the most comfortable approach. Comfort zones place you in a stagnated position, leaving you with nowhere to go. Just like Lot's wife, you become a pillar of salt that only brings back dead memories (See Genesis 19).   Being aware that you're pregnant with purpose should move you into the unknown. It should broaden your vision and increase your momentum. The months I carried my children, I could only think about holding them in my arms. The pregnancy sent me into my future, and the months I carried my son was truly filled with great expectations. This was the son I'd spoken into existence. This was the child I'd called by name out of the realm of the spirit, and into the dispensation of time. My mind never went back to the questions I asked God in the past. Questions like, "Lord, when are you going to release my son into the natural?" Those kinds of questions had no power because the spoken Word had manifested in the natural.

The past means that it no longer exists; it is gone by and it is over. So many times, it is the things that no longer exist that hold us captive. Past relationships bind us to the point of fearing the next one. Yes, my past relationships were very bad experiences, but I can't bring those past hurts into my present life. I can't allow what happened to me back then keep me from reaching into my destiny. It is time we understand that the past is over and it has no power. The past lets us know that we made it through the last fight, we ran through the last race, and we survived the last storm. Our pasts gives us the ability to rejoice because we are still alive. It gives us the power to identify our places in God. Yes, the devil sent wolves after me, but they couldn't take me out! He sent temptation, but God gave me a way of escape! Everything the devil tried in my past wasn't powerful enough to kill me! I know it was my past encounters that gave me my ability to fight now! I thank God for the bad as well as the good. I thank Him for every experience I've walked through on this journey called life. Life takes you down many bumpy and rough roads, but it leads you into a strong and powerful destination. My past did not have the power to determine my future. Even though life threw me some tough blows, I am yet empowered to make a difference in many lives.

I wasn't brought up in a positive environment, I didn't attend the best of schools, I didn't have the best of parents, and I didn't receive the best instructions, but I now surround myself with an environment that will cause me to grow in wisdom, knowledge, and understanding. No, I didn't attend the best of schools, but God is now using me to teach the uncompromising Word of God. I didn't have the best of parents, but I can proudly say that I've been adopted into a royal family. No, I didn't receive the best instructions, but I am now instructed by the all-powerful Word of God. As you can see, my past didn't have the power to determine my future. I'm walking in confidence now. Everything I needed was missing in the beginning, but now that I am in Jesus, nothing is missing and nothing is broken. Even though life's experiences has introduced to me many levels of suffering, God's glory has manifested through it all. Yes, over the years, negative things have surfaced on extreme levels, but the positive has always prevailed. Through it all, God is still glorified in my life, and that is all that matters.

The things that used to puzzle me makes sense now. My life was once filled with discouragement. There were times when I didn't want to face the next day, but now, I look forward to every day. I realize that each day, I am growing closer to my destiny. Destiny is drawing me to build on all the pain and abuse I've experienced throughout my life. I can truly say that I am empowered by my past, numb to my present state, and determined to step into my future. There is nothing powerful enough to hold me captive. I am free to step into my season to enjoy all God has for me.

Present means existing now; your current state. This is a powerful place because now, you have the opportunity to determine your future. We have gone through tests and trials, and now, we have the experience. We have been given the information we need to respond correctly to the storms of life. I consider myself to be numb to the things that the enemy throws at me now. I realize that the things that occur now are subject to change at any time. So, just as my past couldn't determine where I am now, neither can the present trials determine my future.

I believe God has to constantly stir our hearts back into the visions and dreams He has promised. I will never forget the season He began reminding me to embrace everything He had promised me. Tests and trials had hit my life and my emotions overshadowed every promise God had given me. It was my job to hold fast to what God had spoken, regardless of what I was facing at that present moment. God had to let me know I had the ability to magnify the promise, regardless of the present conditions. He had to stir my ability to change my thinking. Once my thinking changed, so did my language.

My negative thinking had manifested a life I had never dreamed of. My marriage had completely ended. The divorce papers were signed and my husband and I were living in different states. My present state was horrible; every hope I had concerning my family seemed to be pointless. Nevertheless, I was traveling down a road to reach my final destination, and I couldn't let anything abort the promise. God reassured me that He was still able to manifest the promise, and I can proudly say that my present state does not have the power to determine my future. My husband returned home and we proudly renewed our vows. God manifested the promise, and all I had to do was remain focused on what I wanted God to do.

Future means something that will happen. Our total focus should be on the vision that God has given us. The promises of God should have the power to build us up from past situations and pull us through our present states. We should spend every moment of our lives praying for creative ideas that will assure us a successful end. We survived our pasts to embrace our futures. The trials we're facing now are empowering us to step into everything God has for us. We must go through the storm and the rain to receive our abundant lives, and we must know that our past fights were organized to teach us to fight the good fight of faith.

Empowered to Witness

To the weak (wanting in discernment) I have become weak (wanting in discernment) that I might win the weak and over scrupulous. I have [in short] become all things to all men that I might by all means (at all costs and in any and every way) save some (by winning them to faith in Jesus Christ (1 Corinthians 9:22 Amp).

I realize that when God created me, He put everything I

needed to survive on the inside of me. I know this long and hard journey was all a part of His plan for me. This is the way God expects us to view our lives. God is saying, *"For Shelia to know that she can endure, I must allow her to go through some things that most people would die going through. I have to allow her to see some things that would cause most people to lose hope if they witnessed. I have to allow her to experience some things so she will be empowered to minister through her experience. If I don't work the prayer warrior out of her, she'll never know she's anointed to pray without ceasing. I have to allow her to step into time experiencing chaos to prepare her for the fights of the 21st century. I have to allow her to grow up in a very dysfunctional family so she can minister to other dysfunctional people."* God was always preparing me, and He had to allow certain things to take place in my life so that victory may spring forth. I understand that everything I've faced in this life was a part of God's plan for my life. My alcoholic parents were part of the plan. My abusive father was a part of the plan. Having a child out of wedlock was a part of the plan. I went through all of that to be anointed for this day and time. I realize that experience is the best teacher. I now understand that I wouldn't be boldly walking in this apostolic anointing had I not experienced the things I have.

Through a journey of ups and downs, God has given

me a strong witness. I believe I have experienced adversity in its deepest form, and through it all, God has given me a ministry of reconciliation. He has imparted strength to me through the things I once thought could destroy me. The mind-boggling things that were a sure sign that I was only moments away from having a nervous breakdown were used to give me the mind of Christ. The tests and trials that were powerful enough to cause me to throw in the towel were used to empower me. Everything the enemy used to destroy me made me a better representative of Christ. I can truly say that purpose keeps you even when it seems like life's circumstances are taking you out. I was born with purpose, created for destiny, anointed to stand, equipped to fight, and empowered to live eternally for Christ. There's nothing powerful enough to cause me to lose hope. I know my Creator lives and He dwells richly on the inside of me.

Every fight I've ever fought was for someone else. Every struggle I forced my way through was created for someone else. I was created to make a difference in someone else's life. I wasn't the target: the harvest of souls I'm anointed to win were. The enemy knows and recognizes that I have been empowered to snatch souls out of the clutches of his deceptive grip. His goal has always been to pressure me into giving up because then he wants to get more souls to join him in hell. We really can't begin to understand how important it is that we stand, represent

the Lord, fight, and never ever give up. It is time for us to
see the lives that have been given into our hands, and the
souls God has anointed us to reach.

I am on a run for Jesus because I have come into the
knowledge of my purpose. I realize I was born to make a
difference in many lives. I know I must live so others may
have life. I went through the tests that I may help someone
else past those same tests. The trials have never been about
me; they were for every reader who purchases this book,
every sick person who receives their healing, and every
intercessor who embraces prayer. No, it wasn't about me,
but it was always about the difference I would make in
other people lives.

I can't explain where I am in God; all I know is I've
never been here before. His presence is overwhelming and
His power is breathtaking. He's bringing friends back into
my life who truly need my testimony. I now understand
why I was attacked so vigorously. I now understand why I
was labeled as everything except a child of God. I
understand why I was kicked around like trash. I couldn't
understand it then, but now, I know that it was only a part
of the process. Watching my stepmother get abused by my
father was traumatic, and because of what I saw, I believed
I would never allow myself to suffer to that extreme. The
very thing I said I wouldn't do was the very thing I found

myself bound to. I had to learn that Jesus is the only way out. There is no way we can walk out of bondage without having Jesus walking with us. There is no way we can talk our way out of bondage without having the power of God's Word. There is no way we can think outside of a carnal mind without having the knowledge, wisdom, and understanding of God. We are bound to whatever life sends our way if we never embrace Jesus.

I now have hope because I chose to place my hope in Jesus. I now have peace because I've allowed the peace of God to rule in my heart. I now have victory over life's circumstances only because Jesus has made me to triumph over my enemies. I now have love because Jesus is love and He dwells richly on the inside of me. If I wouldn't have embraced Jesus with all of my heart, I wouldn't be free now. I am now free from every yoke of bondage, every trap that the enemy set to entrap and kill me. I am free from every stronghold of the mind. Jesus's blood has redeemed me, and I am proud to say my life reflects it. Everyone who knows me wouldn't have thought in a million years that Shelia Taylor would be ministering God's Word and living by precept and example. I am who I am only by the blood of the lamb, and nothing or no one can separate me from the love of God.

I've walked through some hard times, and because I

survived those trials, I must witness to God's people. I feel like there is not enough that I can do to express my gratitude to God for saving me. I have given Him my all because He gave me His all. I must die to sin because He died that I may walk in righteousness. I can't see myself making a public disgrace of Jesus. I must serve Him wholeheartedly; I refuse to crucify Him all over again. The Bible informs us in Hebrews 6:4-6 (Amp), "It is impossible [to restore and bring again to repentance] those who have been once for all enlightened, who have consciously tasted the heavenly gift and have become sharers of the Holy spirit, And have felt how good the Word of God is and the mighty powers of the age and world to come, If they then deviate from the faith and turn away from their allegiance-[it is impossible] to bring them back to repentance, for (because, while, as long as) they nail upon the cross the Son of God afresh [as far as they are concerned] and are holding [Him] up to contempt and shame and public disgrace."

The Word lets us know that regardless of what we're being faced with, we must truly represent God in this earth realm. In the midst of trials, we can sometimes find it hard to understand why we have to go through certain things, but the seasons of hardship should usher us into the presence of God. We should learn to abide in peace, even if our surroundings aren't peaceful. God is trying to teach us that storms are produced only to make us better. Every test and trial is transforming us into the instruments we were born to be. I wouldn't have thought in a million years that my marriage would end and be restored again in less than a year, but I must admit that during the separation, I began to see myself in ways that I refused to see when my husband and I were together. So, the marriage ended and the divorce papers were signed, but it all worked together for my good. Because of my life's experiences, I am empowered to witness, and I am also able to say with all certainty that all things work together for good to them that love God, to them who are called according to His purpose (Romans 8:28).

My Prayer for You

I pray that you will have the ability to know that your fights are a part of God's preordained plan for you. I also pray you will accept what God allows in every season. It doesn't matter what tests, trials, or hardships you may face, God is in control. Your past, present, and future are in the hands of God. He is the potter and you are the clay. I pray that you will allow Him to mold you into the vessel you were created to be, causing you to function properly for His perfect will. It is my prayer that you will be built up in such a way that will cause you to only release truth. Through it all, I pray God will speedily perfect those things that concern you, and that you will be an effective witness

for this day and time.
In Jesus Name,
Amen.

Chapter 14

Manifesting the Fullness of the Gift

Do not neglect the gift which is in you [that special inward endowment] which was directly imparted to you [by the Holy Spirit] by prophetic utterance when the elders laid their hands upon you [at your ordination]. Practice and activate and meditate upon these duties, throw yourself wholly unto them [as your ministry] so that your progress may be evident to everybody (1 Timothy 4:14-15 Amp).

The year I returned to Memphis, God began speaking to me in a very profound way. He was commanding me to hear His voice and obey His instructions. He had done great things for me back home, and there was a level of warfare raging up against my life that couldn't be ignored. I moved to Memphis thinking I was going to rest, but God continued to direct my attention back to my assignment. My obedience in starting The Anointed Gap Standers' Ministries elevated me into new realms of authority, and even though I was totally aware of my position in the kingdom, disobedience caused my exalted position to be limited.

God was constantly commanding me to step out on faith and continue the assignment He had placed on my life. Admittedly, I kept joining different ministries hoping that someone would help TAGS Ministries, but to no avail. I had allowed the opinions of others to slow me down for years. God made it clear that I didn't need anyone in the natural to help me do what He had already anointed me to do. God continued to show me that my assignment was too serious to be ignored. He made it clear that it was time for me to embrace the fullness of my assignment. I was certain that I didn't have a problem with obeying God, but my previous experiences made me want to do things a little differently. I stepped out on faith to start my ministry back home and created enemies like never before, but regardless of my limited thinking, God made it clear that I didn't need anyone in the natural. He sent me back to unfamiliar territory so I would only have Him to turn to. On Judgment Day, I will not be able to point fingers at the men and women who wouldn't help me. God is going to deal with me concerning the instructions He has given me. Excuses cannot stand before a Holy God, only the truth. God knows my ability to hear Him, and my faith must take on legs and get busy in this earth realm. I know that as each day passes, destiny is still patiently waiting on me to step into it. Life is fleeting, and I'm going to be held accountable for all my actions. Over the years, I've watched myself gaze into the eyes of spiritual leaders. I was drawn to them with the hope that they would do more for me. I was stagnated in ministry because I had placed my God given assignment in the hands of man. I now realize that the thing I'm called to do is designed for me. No man in this earth realm can see my assignment like I can. There is not a soul alive who's capable of giving me my steps to success. For years, I'd allowed man to hinder me from releasing my true identity. I know that my faith is the only thing that will reward me with the fullness of who I am. We must know that the beauty of who we are was placed there for a purpose. The anointing God has given us was given for kingdom works. There are souls waiting on the abundance of the gift, and it is time to embrace the fullness of who you are. You must understand that embracing who you are rewards not only you, but also the many souls who are depending on the power that is released through you. I couldn't ignore God's instructions during that time. He spoke to me through everything, and He was very clear with His instructions. He placed a command on me to step out on faith and to use what I had. I didn't completely understand what God was instructing me to use, so I asked Him to bring clarity to the instructions. He then gave me a vision of my dining room. I was instructed to start TAGS Ministries in the comfort of my own home. Once God's instructions were given, I could no longer use the excuse of having no resources. I was given vision and provision, but I still allowed the darkness of my past experiences to stagnate me. There was a serious assignment on the inside of me, but it was so hard for me to obey God because of the torments of my past. The experiences I'd endured in my hometown were truly boot-camp for ministry. There was an apostle on the inside hiding, but God knew what office He'd anointed me to walk in. The command was clear, but it was so hard to embrace the assignment without being attacked by the enemy. It appeared as if I was being robbed tremendously in my personal life. I returned to my old ministry with a mind to rest, but the attacks kept me in warfare mode. I felt as if the enemy had robbed me of my will to obey God. Over the years, I had fought the good fight of faith for my ministry, but I had reached a moment in time that fighting was the furthest thing from my mind. It is so important that you hold fast to the dreams and purposes God has placed within you. If God put purpose in you, know that it is bigger than you and bigger than how you may feel at that moment. Greatness involves helping others, and so many people are waiting on your obedience. I didn't know how important it was that the apostle in me be released. I didn't know until God began to bring other strong women into my life. You know, we find ourselves limiting our ability to function in the kingdom of God because of gender, but please know that our God is not prejudiced, and He is no respecter of persons. God had spoken through many men in the past, confirming that I was called to be an apostle in the earth realm, but it wasn't until He allowed me to meet Apostle Tina Edwards that I began to wake up. She was not called to cover TAGS Ministries, neither was she called to mentor me. God used an apostle to stir up an apostle. She demonstrated how to release the power of God, and she was the first person I had come into contact with who had seen the glimpse of my anointing from within, and commanded it to come out. God used her to do for me what I had done for others. She stirred my ability to run again. TAGS Ministries began to stand up in me in such a way that I couldn't hold it in any longer. Through this vessel of God, my gifting began to surface again. It felt as if I had been picked up in a whirlwind and dropped in a place called destiny. My life has never been the same. God used this woman of God to place running in my feet, and I've been getting the job done ever since.

I know that I'm on my way! The work of the kingdom is in progress, and I'm boldly positioning myself. The first night I visited Apostle Tina Edward's ministry, one of her ministers released a word entitled Transition into Position. This word spoke volumes to my life. I had been transitioning into ministries, releasing the anointing into the visions of others, and ignoring my own. My anointing had been released, but not for the position God had empowered me for.

The difference between Apostle Tina Edward and leaders from my past is that she had the ability to shoot my spirit to the place it needed to be for my own assignment. I believe that through Apostle Tina Edward, my spirit was commanded to pick up the pace again. It was something done for me in the spirit that caused me to run in the natural. I know that I am on my way; my ministry is moments away from being one of the greatest soul-winning ministries in the world. My book, the one you are reading now, is about to jump off the charts. I am being prepared to be recognized as one of God's best-selling authors. My assignment is in progress now, and God is connecting me with His people from all over the world! A serious network is forming now in Jesus name. No, this is not arrogance, but it is a prophetic word, and I challenge you to watch God because He is going to manifest these spoken words right before your eyes. God is not a man that He should lie. He said it, I believe it, and He is performing it even now, in Jesus name.

Following All of God's Instructions

[That you may really come] to know [practically, through experience for yourselves] the love of Christ, which far surpasses mere knowledge, [without experience], that you may be filled [through all your being] unto all the fullness of God [may have the richest measure of the divine Presence, and become a body wholly filled and flooded with God Himself] (Ephesians 3:19 Amp).

Over the years, I've learned the importance of obeying God in every season. Timing is an important factor when it comes to kingdom work. God is waiting for our acts of obedience, and through our obedience, He connects us with people who will help bring the vision to pass. I can remember the time God commanded me to write this book. Writing was something that came as natural as washing my face. He didn't tell me what to write or how much to write. In obedience, I began jotting down thoughts and situations, and my life's experiences rapidly became a book entitled *Embracing Intercession Through Life's Experiences*.

The promise manifested in the natural only because I maintained a focused mind. I didn't have to ponder the name of this book. My obedience produced great results, and I learned that all God needed was a willing vessel. He needed an instrument who would trust Him enough to follow all of His instructions. God will get all of the glory, and our ability to step out on the impossible eventually gives us the ability to see in the realm of the spirit. Once our faith pushes us out on nothing, God gives us the ability to walk on water. For God to reveal more of His plans for our lives, faith must become the moving force. It was impossible for me to complete the assignment that God had given me without the help of others, but my obedience introduced me to my proofreader, editor, and publisher. God is a God of order, and we must obey the first set of instructions to get the rest of the instructions. We must move with God to maintain a constant momentum. Our thoughts and ways are not as God's, but our obedience uncovers and reveals the mysteries of God. I felt like I needed to know who would publish my book before I started writing. God was saying, "Obey the instructions and I will uncover along the way." Through my writings, God began to teach me how important it was that I flowed with Him. God has gifted me in the areas of writing and interceding, and at all times, I must function according to His leading in both gifts. Writing seems to keep you in a progressive movement. As one thought is released, you find yourself releasing new thoughts. As you give yourself more and more to the gift, you can't help but to accept the beauty of being a profound writer. It's amazing how you seem to not only own the gift, but you become the gift. I often find myself viewing myself as an author, an intercessor, and a leader. For me to become fully developed in the call that is upon my life, I must flow with the Spirit of God. As we obey God in the small things, He rewards us with greater things. Obedience has rewarded me with the privilege of seeing myself as God sees me. Just as there is a progressive movement in writing, there is a progressive movement in intercession, and it can't be compared to anything in the natural. Jesus stood in the gap on the behalf of all mankind, giving us the ability to be used as temples of God. We have become dwelling places who release God's will into the earth realm. Intercession is a swift movement of God. This supernatural move has a unique way of manifesting God's will for natural eyes to see, and once we make the decision to give ourselves to intercession, the demonstrations of God's miracles become a norm.

The manifestation of the vision will appear only through hearing and obeying the instructions of God. TAGS Ministries wasn't uncovered until I obeyed God in the small things. My faithfulness over the small things propelled me to start my own prayer ministry. Through every step, I began to tap into the mystery of who I was. I stepped out because there was a command on my spirit. As I moved into the things of God, great things surfaced. I was able to see the rapid hand of God through every faith move. He moved speedily through my obedience, and I am now enjoying the benefits of following all of the instructions.

I walked into the now season of my life using what I had. I didn't have a building, but I had a living room. We gathered together, and everyone who understood the unity concept, transitioned with me into a conference room within a four week period. We sent invitations out to different local ministries in the city, inviting them to join us for our first prayer gathering. God used faith moves only to introduce me to a greater level of intercession. Once a strong foundation of intercession was laid for the prayer ministry, God instructed us to gain more territory by walking the city. I couldn't get caught up on my own agenda. Yes, I wanted a building and I wanted to see the manifestation of everything He had promised, but God was teaching me how important kingdom work was. It wasn't about being confined to four walls. God had placed a serious anointing on my ministry, and He wanted me to understand that my ministry was within me and not within a set building. TAGS Ministries is much more than a set house. It is a constant movement of God, therefore, I must keep my desires out of the way. God has taught me that all He needs is my obedience, and He would do the rest. I was never allowed to release questions after a command. It was my job to hear and move. I felt how Noah may have felt while building the ark. All he had were instructions, and regardless of the voices around him, he couldn't stop building. I know to the natural eye, TAGS Ministries appears unstable, but I am commanded to move with God. A glory cloud is leading me, and I can't allow a natural crowd to discourage me. I know my ability to hear and obey. No, I'm not sure when the fullness of the vision will manifest, but I'm certain that it will manifest as long as I obey all of the instructions. I am certain of this one thing:

He who has begun a good work in me will continue unto the coming of Christ. I am certain, without a doubt, that God will continue to work for His kingdom through my obedience.

My Prayer for You

I pray that my life's experiences have stirred your inner man in such a way that sitting on purpose has been done away with. I pray that the boldness of who you are is being presented to the nations of this world and that God is only moments away from giving you your increase. I pray that every chapter in this book has either planted or watered something in your life, and that purpose is springing up out of you like a flowing fountain. I pray that your head is lifted up and your confidence level is reaching the clouds. Know that everything that hindered you in the past has been demolished in Jesus name, and that you are swiftly running in the right direction, drawing closer and closer to the place called destiny. I pray you keep running, and that you refuse to give up, realizing that you have a finished work and it is waiting on you. So, my friend, I prophesy that your preordained assignment is only moments away from being presented to the nations of the world.
In Jesus Name,
Amen.

Conclusion Presenting the Finished Work

Better is the end of a thing than the beginning of it and the patient in Spirit is better than the proud in spirit (Ecclesiastes 7:8 Amp.).

What an accomplishment! Regardless of the struggles and heartaches I've faced, I can proudly say *I did it.* I can rejoice now because the struggle is over. No longer am I trying to get my ministry off the ground, but I am going forth in Jesus name. No longer am I trying to complete my first book, but it is hitting the bookstores and being purchased by friends and family all over the world. I have reached a milestone in my life, and I can proudly look back and see the importance of my journey. The negative words that were released to hinder my progress in the kingdom don't matter anymore. I have completed a God-given task, and the voices that surrounded me couldn't stop me. My adversary, the devil, has lost the battle again. God is on my side, and He's speaking directly to my spirit: *Well done, my child, well done!* I encourage every reader to keep running because your reward is at the finished line, waiting on you to get there.

The devil didn't mind me starting TAGS Ministries, as long as I didn't finish. I must say that starting an assignment is easy; the challenge is in maintaining the assignment that is given. Experience has taught me the importance of not giving up. God will reward me for my diligence; He would never reward me for giving up. I can see my promised land, but getting there is my real success. We should never get stuck in the beginning of a thing because God is Alpha and Omega, the Beginning and the End. He is the Author and the Finisher of our faith. He didn't stop creating until the day of completion. Jesus didn't come down off the cross until He was able to release, "It is finished!" So we can't stop seeing and creating until the day of completion.

Leaders, God has given us callings and assignments because of our ability to finish. He places endurance in His spiritual leaders. Throwing in the towel is never a part of the process. If God has given you a beginning, you must continue to strive until you see your end. My assignment was packed with challenges, but without the obstacles, I wouldn't have had enough experiences to write this book. To write a book entitled, *Embracing Intercession through Life's Experiences*, God had to place me in real battles. Through those battles, God taught me how to survive the storms of life, and He granted me revelation that I may impart that revelation into His creation. Excuses couldn't reward me, and there was no power in giving up. The power was in my being able to stand through it all. Being able to endure has rewarded me with the completion of this book and the manifestation of The Anointed Gap Standers'

Ministries.

Now that I have completed this book, I'm able to reap the benefits of completion, and the fact that I didn't allow excuses or the opinions of others to keep me from starting TAGS Ministries is a reflection of my faith. I can now proclaim that my feet are planted firmly on the path that leads to my destiny. Excuses are done away with and obedience has taken precedence over everything else. I've snatched my purpose out of the hands of others, and I'm on my way to my promised land. I'm running free of the distractions that once slowed me down. I'm not looking around, waiting on the opinions of others. I know that destiny is waiting on me, and because I can see it, I've chosen to take wide stride and swifter steps. I've decided to run at a pace that rewards me with the prize. I've made up my mind, and I have fully grasped the reins. I'm no longer shackled by the bondage of disbelief and doubt. I believe the promise, I believe I can have it, I believe that I'm capable of receiving it as heaven's reward.

Everything in my life is changing for the better, especially my language. Since God has given me the ability to speak, I choose to speak the words that will produce fruit in my life. No longer will I change my language because it is too weighty for others. No longer will I change my stride because others can't keep up. No longer will I fail to see the greatness because others fail to see the benefits that come with living a righteous life. God has promised me victory through His Son's finished work. He has created me with purpose in mind, and He has made that purpose clear to me. I now have sense enough to know that I was born to complete the assignment that God has shown me. So, watch out nations of the world! God is launching someone new! All the limitations have been taken off, and nothing in this earth realm is powerful enough to keep me from my finished work!

64977528R00137

Made in the USA
Charleston, SC
11 December 2016